HOW TO REPROGRAM YOURSELF FOR SUCCESS

Everton Weekes

Please note that the author capitalizes certain words in Scripture that refer to God the Father, the Son, and the Holy Spirit, and may differ from some Bible publisher's style. Take note that the name satan and related names are not capitalized. The author chooses not to recognize him, even to the point of violating grammatical regulations.

Cover design by Steve Stanczyk www.stevestanczyk.com www.xulonpress.com.

www.xulonpress.com

Dedication

I dedicate this book to those who want to make their lives more beautiful and meaningful, and to those who think their dreams are impossible.

I also devote this book to those who will accept the challenge to do what it takes to be a success; to those who will set their minds on the prize, so their dreams can become reality.

The words on these pages are dedicated to those who feel alone and without personal value. I wrote this book with you in mind.

Finally, I dedicate this book to my mother. Mom, I love you so much. Thank you for teaching me the true value of the riches of life. You were the embodiment of thankfulness, and because of you I can say, I AM RICH!

Acknowledgements

A special thanks to my Man of God, Apostle Charles Ndifon. From the first day I saw you in Vancouver, B.C., Canada, I knew it was an appointment with destiny. Your discerning heart is one of your greatest gifts from God. You saw gold in my wife and I, and you mined for it. You saw a calling and you mentored it. You saw a ministry and you released it. You are a modern day Elijah who is not afraid to share, and bring others into your inheritance. Thank you for your love, wisdom, and the anointing that you and your lovely wife, Donna, have imparted into us. Our lives are truly indebted to you both. Thank you for not only being my man of God, but also a close friend and confidante.

Special thanks to all my leadership and staff, and every member of the Living Faith Miracle Centers. Thank you for running the race with Pastor Tracy and I. Life on earth would be very difficult without you.

Thanks to my editorial team: Karen, Vanessa, Danielle and Neil, who have diligently typed, edited and reworked my many words. Thank you for polishing it, and turning it into a weapon in the hands of the Holy Spirit. I could not have asked for a better support team in the world.

Last, but certainly not least, I extend my love to our four beloved children: Elijah, Michaelah, Joshua and Christianna. All four of you are miracle children. You are my greatest joy. I am so proud of all of you. Remember God created you for success, and your success is linked to all the great gifts He has placed in you.

Table of Contents

Endorsement

What a great honor and joy it is for us to write this acknowledgment for this wonderful man of God, who has become a very precious friend to us. It has blessed and motivated us immensely to see over the years how he has constantly stirred up his love and faith in Papa God. He passionately pursues all the great promises Jesus gave. It's no wonder that Jesus has blessed his apostolic ministry with great signs and wonders.

The yearly conferences we have with him and his wife have brought us as a church into new dimensions and blessed us tremendously. Every time Apostle and Pastor Tracy leave our church after a conference, our people are already looking forward to the next time they come. Under his anointed, powerful teaching, people receive heavenly keys to be able to experience God's promises in their lives. The driving force of his actions and behaviors are pure love and passion for God and the people. When he ministers, he forgets the time and gives 100% of himself away to the needy people. It is touching to see!

In the same way that Papa God Himself flows through his anointed son Everton, He will touch your heart while you are reading this book. Revelation will hit you and you will be catapulted in new dimensions, while you get reprogrammed according to Papa God's software. So, we encourage you to begin the journey to reprogram yourself for success!

Hartmut & Marietta Olschewsky
Senior Pastors, *Touch the Love Ministries*

Foreword

I am honored to write this forward for one of my dearest and best friends, Everton Weekes.

In life, things may happen to you that cause you to believe you can't make it. Circumstances and pressures can keep you back, and if allowed to, swallow up your dreams. However, this book will encourage you that it's possible to break through all of these forces! With God, you can become who you were destined to become. You can and will rise above the negativity of life, and be God's voice and healing touch to a dying world!

I have known Everton for over a decade now, and have witnessed firsthand the touch of God upon his life, his wife and his family. With pure motivation and devotion, Everton lets you know that through God you can do valiantly! God is not a respecter of persons, and He can do the same with you. Everton travels the nations preaching the gospel and demonstrating the power of God. The sick are healed and lives are changed for the glory of God. However, more than that, what I love about Everton is that he demonstrates this love to his wife and family. He loves them, and he loves God's people, whoever and wherever they are!

Be encouraged by this book, and let your life soar into the greatest future God has designed, just for you!

Brad Alford Senior Pastor *New Day Center*
Paso Robles, California

Introduction

Our Stories - From Ashes to Beauty
by Everton and Tracy Weekes

"**S**ticks and stones can break my bones but words will never hurt me." Those were my thoughts as a child. I only wish they were true. Today I have come to realize that words have life and personality. Words create seasons and events! Words shape and dictate destinies. Words are seeds for feelings and also for pain.

I was born in a small village, on a little Caribbean Island called St. Kitts. I still remember the voices of my teachers telling me how dumb I was for not knowing the difference between a verb and noun. Being the youngest of fifteen children was even more disheartening because everything was passed down to me! Being the recipient of hand-me-downs was not always a bad a thing. There were times I thought it was cool; wearing my brothers' yellow jeans and neon green shirt, which in the 70's and 80's were out this world. However, this lifestyle programmed me to think that nothing good or new would ever come to me.

I always thought that the rich kids were the smarter ones, and the chance of them becoming successful was higher than for the poor ones! I did not have great teachers in school, nor did I have Christ-centered role models who would nurture my dreams. As a result of this, satan was able to reinforce the spirit of failure within me. Another way satan scarred my tender soul was through my speech impediment. I could not speak. I was called the dumb, stammering kid in the village! I remember going to bed, wondering what the purpose of life was, and how I could ever overcome the pain of isolation and shame. However, God always has a way out when we trust Him.

By some miraculous event, I was invited to come to Canada, and upon my arrival I encountered a whole new set of problems. I was black in a sea of white faces. Now, being black and living in Canada was not the problem. The problem was me! I was programmed to think second class, wired to be inferior, shaped by a philosophy that nothing good was in me, and nothing great could ever come from me. But thanks be unto God, because of His grace and some wonderful people, I am who I am today.

Child of God, this book was written with you in mind, to mentor and inspire you. Please know that no matter what circumstances you find yourself in, with God's grace you can always rise above them. After over two decades of walking with Jesus, I am convinced that if you put the principles contained in this book to work, your life will never be the same. His grace can also work for you and your family!

By Everton Weekes

Healed from Cancer

My story; His love

"The things my husband is sharing in this book are the principles that have brought healing and restoration to our lives, and to thousands of people around the world who have attended our crusades and life changing conferences. My upbringing was a little different from that of my husband's. I am the oldest of three children and my parents did everything in their power to raise us up in the ways of the Lord."

Then, because of pain I experienced as a child, I tried to numb the hurting with pleasures of the world. But God, in His love and mercy, had the last word and set me free.

I returned to the Lord and vowed to serve Him. Around that same time, I met my Everton, and a year later we were married. I always knew the call on my life was very strong for ministry. In the summer of 1998, we sold all our earthly possessions and left for the USA with our two young children, to train and be discipled by Apostle Charles and Pastor Donna Ndifon.

Everything was going very well, when the unthinkable happened. In the fall of 2000, when I was pregnant with our third child, my doctor told me I had cervical cancer. I was very shaken and upset by this because I was so young, and my other two pregnancies had gone so well.

A medical team told me that I would have to undergo surgery to remove the cancerous cells. As well, they talked about chemotherapy, a hysterectomy, (removal of the womb) and taking my baby a month early by C-section. They said there would be a great chance that the baby's lungs and other organs would not be fully developed.

My husband and I prayed, and changed our thinking. We exchanged the negative doctor's report for the report of the Lord, and His testimony. We were confident that we would see His hand move in our direction. So we prayed together and believed for a good report. It was during this time that a particular Scripture stood out powerfully to me. It was *2 Timothy 1:12b (AMP)* which says, *"For I know (perceive, have knowledge of, and am acquainted with) Him Whom I have believed (adhered to and trusted in and relied on), and I am (positively) persuaded that He is able to guard and keep that which has been entrusted to me and which I have committed (to Him) until that day."*

I had full and total confidence that God wanted me whole just as much as I did, if not more. I came to the point where I was completely persuaded of God's healing power for my life.

My case went before six pathologists for review and a follow-up appointment was set for the next week, when I would get my test results back. When that day came, I walked into the doctor's office and waited for my report. Understandably, I was feeling very apprehensive, but in my spirit I was fully confident that Jesus had healed me.

The doctor sat down and opened my file. She said that after extensively reviewing my case, they could no longer find any trace of cancerous cells. She had no explanation. She was amazed that I was the same young woman whose files she had read only a week prior! She recommended that I take another follow-up test in a month, and that I was free to go! That second test also revealed that I was free from all cancer.

Our son Joshua was born at full term that December. Today he is a strong, healthy, active boy. I thank God every day for what He did for my family. I know He is alive today, and that He loves and cares for each one of us! I am living proof that the principles my husband will share with you work.

We are not sharing these things with you because we have already arrived. No! We still fight to lay hold of that which belongs to us, but it is much easier to fight with knowledge and truth. Child of God, the knowledge in this book is a gold mine and when applied, it can take you places.

We have proven these principles of success in our lives and ministry over and over again. They always work. So now your time has come to shine and be all you were created to be. Get ready to change, increase, and walk in victory so you can be all that God has called you to be.

By Tracy Weekes

CHAPTER ONE

HOW TO REPROGRAM YOURSELF FOR SUCCESS

L ove and anger cannot coexist in one heart, just as two objects cannot occupy the same place at once. You cannot have two cars parked in one spot. Evil and good cannot occupy the same space at the same time. The same is true concerning your thoughts and ideas. In essence, nothing changes until we are changed. A man's life is the product of his knowledge and thoughts, nothing less and nothing more. Consequently, until you change and give up your old way of doing things, your life will keep producing the same old negative results.

Grow Success by Changing Old Images

"The good man from his inner good treasure flings forth good things, and the evil man out of his inner evil storehouse flings forth evil things. But I tell you, on the day of judgment men will have to give account for every idle (inoperative, nonworking) word they speak. For by your words you will be justified and acquitted, and by your words you will be condemned and sentenced." Matthew 12:35-37 (AMP)

The images you hold in your heart determine whether you will fail or succeed in life. A lot of people think God or the devil decide for you how successful you will be. In my opinion, over ninety percent of the problems most people face do not come from the devil. Rather, difficulties arise from the negative images they carry in their minds. Why do they have a negative thought life? Many people have been poorly programmed.

I am going to share some principles with you that God has used to bring tremendous healing to my heart. God has literally taken me from a poor village in the Caribbean to become a successful minister of the gospel today. (In the closing chapter, I will share on some of blessings I received from being raised in poverty, and why I would not trade it for a million dollars.)

If your mind is full of thoughts about shortage, fear, sickness and poverty, success will be slow in coming to you. My friend, for you and I to walk in the victory of Christ, we have to overcome every negative image and mindset. Negativity opens the door for satan to enter our lives and paralyze our God-given potential. That is what happened to Job.

"For the thing which I greatly feared is come upon me, and that which I was afraid of is come unto me" Job 3:25

The English Standard Version of this verse puts it this way: *"For the thing that I fear comes upon me, and what I dread befalls me."*

Repeat with me now, these declarations for a healthy mindset:

"I uproot every negative image inside my mind. Every fear, every shortage and every lack.

I DECLARE THIS DAY that images of abundance, health, favor and success are now growing in me. I root out any seeds of fear, lack, sickness or low self-esteem.

I DECLARE THIS DAY that I am a bundle of success. I am a springboard of joy, and God is helping me and working in me now.

I DECLARE THIS DAY that the wisdom of God is neutralizing and destroying all the plans of satan in my life."

The Image You Behold Is the Image You Become

In the Bible, the children of Israel could not even enter their land of promise because of the negative images they possessed. Their mindsets of slavery, fear and bondage neutralized the power of God working in them. This can also be our fate if we choose not to change any negative programming we may have. Years ago, a young man came to my office seeking prayer for his problem. His problem was, he could never hold down a job for more than six months, and his life went from crisis to crisis. He believed he was under a curse, and as I listened to him, I came to the same conclusion. Yes, his life was under a curse, but not a curse from satan. The curse was a result of wrong thoughts and images in his mind. This opened the door for the little devil to come in. Child of God, we have to come into agreement with what the Bible says concerning this little devil. The Scriptures tell us that satan is eternally defeated in the life of a child of God, and the Scriptures cannot be broken.

"For this purpose the Son of God was manifested, that He might destroy the works of the devil." 1 John 3:8b

"And having spoiled principalities and powers, He made a shew of them openly, triumphing over them in it." Colossians 2:15

"We know that whosoever is born of God sinneth not; but he that is begotten of God keepeth himself, and that wicked one toucheth him not." 1 John 5:18

The Image of God in You

The images a person looks at are magnetic. They either attract the power of God, or the power of darkness into that individual's life.

Negative images will not disappear just because you are born again. First, you must dispossess them with the blood of Jesus. Then, you must actively and repeatedly replace those images with the Word of God. This is how your life begins to transform. One of the many reasons why God gave you His Word is so that you can begin to create images of success.

Even though the Word of God was spoken and recorded over two thousand years ago, it still contains the same miraculous power, faith and life as when God first spoke it. His Word is alive, and can still bring about changes like it did for God in the beginning.

In the beginning, God used His Word to create and repair His world. We can do the same if we plant the seed of God's Word in our hearts, and water it with our prayers. It will always produce His image and His greatness in us.

Everything God can Do, His Word can Do

How does this work? The first thing you need to understand is the principle of the Inner Image. God thinks in terms of images, and without one, He seldom does anything. In Genesis chapter one, God Himself gives us our first lesson. Here we see Him using the *Inner Image* principle to create the earth He wanted. God did not just come upon creation by accident. God designed it intentionally , just like an architect would have done. He first had a desired result, (an inner idea, or image, of what He wanted to create).

God then said, "Light be!" and light was. He also used the *Inner Image* principle when preparing man to have dominion and control over earth. God placed His Image, the image and DNA of dominion, inside Adam. Why was this so important? You cannot control your outer world if your inner world is in disarray. Knowing this, God in His infinite wisdom placed His own Image inside of man; the image of Lordship and Ruler-ship. With this powerful DNA, man is able to govern his world, just like God governs His Heavens.

What Type of Images Are in You?

I will bring this truth a little closer to home. The Bible is a book of miracles, and is full of miracle word seeds. When you speak those seeds with your mouth and plant them in your heart, you will reap a harvest according to the word seeds you spoke, or planted. If you plant healing seeds, your heart will produce a harvest of healing. If you plant seeds of favor, your heart will produce favor in your life.

Words are spiritual containers that can carry faith, hope and love. They can also carry fear, and even death. Words are so important, they can determine our eternal destiny. *Romans 10:9* says, *"That if thou shalt confess with thy mouth the Lord Jesus, and shalt believe in thine heart that God hath raised Him from the dead, thou shalt be saved."*

Also, *Proverbs 18:21* states, *"Death and life are in the power of the tongue."*

You can use words to transfer spiritual substance from inside your spirit to the outer, natural world. Never underestimate the power of your words and your tongue. Just because you cannot see something in the natural, does not mean it is not real. Think about electricity, magnetism or gravity. These are all very real forces, and if you ignored them or used them the wrong way, they could bring you a lot of trouble. Child of God, if you can see the image of success, prosperity and favor in your spirit, that means they already exist. Now, with the power of your words, you can speak them into the earth. The more you speak, the more you plant the heavenly realm in your world.

"And I have put My Words in thy mouth, and I have covered thee in the shadow of Mine hand, that I may plant the heavens." Isaiah 51:16

"Then the LORD put forth His hand, and touched my mouth. And the LORD said unto me, Behold, I have put My Words in thy mouth. See, I have this day set thee over the nations and over the kingdoms, to root out, and to pull down, and to destroy, and to throw down, to build, and to plant." Jeremiah 1:9-10

Planting New Images of Success

When the Word of God is in your mouth and you speak it out consistently, it will eventually get into your heart. When that happens, the Word will always produce the image of God in you. Once you have the image of God in you, anything that God can do, you can do! The Bible tells us that when the Spirit of God entered into Saul, he became another man, (*1 Samuel 10:6*). The same can be said of you; when the Word of God enters into you, you will also become another person. Lack will become plenty, sickness will become health, bondage will become freedom, and fear will turn into courage!

When the Word becomes flesh in you, you will be as bold as Jesus. Nothing will be impossible to you! So let the Word keep coming out of your mouth. As you do this, I can see changes coming to you in Jesus Name!

26

You cannot live beyond your inner image.
Your inner image controls your life.

Look at what God did with Joshua. Joshua was about to fill the shoes of Moses, a man who literally walked with almighty God – a man who saw God face to face. Joshua had images of fear and intimidation in his mind, which God knew would prevent him from being the leader Israel needed. That is why God had to change the images inside Joshua, so he could be all God called him to be.

You must do the same. You cannot live beyond your inner image, because that is what controls your life. Images of lack, fear and shortage will keep you in the land of limitation. You have to change every negative inner image if you desire to fulfill your destiny. How can you accomplish this? By using the principles that I am teaching you in this chapter.

This is so powerful, I pray you catch it! Remember – the image you behold is the image you become. Never forget that! That is why, in the first chapter of Joshua, God told Joshua to not let the Book of the Law, (God's Word) depart out of his mouth. When God speaks, His Words are full of faith, life, and images of possibility. He told Joshua, *"No man shall be able to stand before you all the days of your life. As I was with Moses, so I will be with you; I will not fail you or forsake you. Be strong (confident) and of good courage, for you shall cause this people to inherit the land which I swore to their fathers to give them. Only you be strong and very courageous, that you may do according to all the law which Moses My servant commanded you. Turn not from it to the right hand or to the left, that you may prosper wherever you go. This Book of the Law shall not depart out of your mouth, but you shall meditate on it day and night, that you may observe and do according to all that is written in it. For then you shall make your way prosperous, and then you shall deal wisely and have good success," (Joshua 1:5-8, AMP).*

Joshua put those words in his mouth, and began to speak them. As a result, the power in those words began to change his inner image. God told him to meditate, which means to think, mutter, and visualize on His Word day and night. Why? *"That [he] may observe and do according to all that is written in it. For then [he] shall make [his] way prosperous, and then [he] shall deal wisely and have good success," (Joshua 1:8 AMP).* This is so powerful! Do you know why?

The word observe means to watch with the intent to see. God wants you and I to meditate until our eyes are opened to see the wondrous things in His Word, *(see Psalm 119:18).* God was telling Joshua that if he would meditate on the Word day and night, he would get an image of that Word inside him. Joshua needed that image. He was about to lead an entire nation. Joshua could not afford to see himself as a loser, or even simply as an ordinary man. He had to become what God intended him to be by meditating on the Word of God. God promised that if Joshua would do that, He would make him wise, prosperous, and successful.

Seven Positive Images To Reprogram Yourself for Success

When images of God's ways enter your spirit, they always release the faith of God. With His faith, you can do anything! However, until any images of fear, bondage or failure are removed from your thinking, your faith potential can never be released.

So my friend, are you ready to go on a journey that will change your life forever? I want to share with you seven positive images that have changed my life. These are the images that have made me who I am today. Please take time to allow these images to grow in your heart, so you can become all you were meant to be. When I give these power seeds to you, you will be like Thomas Edison. Someone once asked him how he was able to give the world so many inventions. His response was, "Because I never think in words, I think in pictures."

Remember – the image you behold is the image that grows in you. The God that you know is the God who will visit you. God revealed Himself throughout history by seven redemptive Names. Each of these Names shows a unique aspect of the Lord in His relationship to His people.

All seven redemptive Names carry powerful images of His Nature. When these Names, or images of what God is like, take root in the soil of your heart, they become like a mighty tree that satan cannot uproot. I often tell my congregation that it is much easier for satan to destroy a seed than a tree. That is why his biggest quest is to stop the seed of God's Word from becoming a strong tree in your life.

1. Jehovah Jireh–The Lord our Provider

Material blessings are redemptive blessings paid for us by Christ's death on the cross.

"For ye know the grace of our Lord Jesus Christ, that, though He was rich, yet for your sake He became poor, that ye through His poverty might be rich." 2 Corinthians 8:9

"He that spared not His own Son, but delivered Him up for us all, how shall He not with Him also freely give us all things?" Romans 8:32

Let this image be so strong in you that all hell starts taking note. My friend, when you become a child of God, you enter into a covenant with Almighty God. He now becomes responsible to take care of all your needs, like any responsible father would. Please do not fight me on this one because we have six more redemptive Names to go! Your Father in Heaven wants you to have more than enough. He is committed to make that happen when you obey Him.

"But if anyone does not provide for his own, and especially for those of his household, he has denied the faith and is worse than an unbeliever." 1 Timothy 5:8 (NKJV)

This is very touching. God is saying that if I, as a father, cannot adequately take care of my family, He sees me as worse than an unbeliever! Now, because all truth is parallel, God lives by that same truth, and provides for His children. Would it not be very hypocritical of Him to expect me to live by this truth if He does not, Himself? God is a loving Father Who is committed to bring His Word to pass in our lives when we practice it.

"And God is able to make all grace (every favor and earthly blessing) come to you in abundance, so that you may always and under all circumstances and whatever the need, be self-sufficient [possessing enough to require no aid or support and furnished in abundance for every good work and charitable donation]." 2 Corinthians 9:8 (AMP)

This is His covenant of provision for you: *"So don't be afraid, little flock. For it gives your Father great happiness to give you the Kingdom," Luke 12:32 (NLT)*

What is in His kingdom? *"The silver is Mine and the gold is Mine, declares the LORD Almighty," Haggai 2:8 (NIV)*

"And my God will meet all your needs according to the riches of His glory in Christ Jesus." Philippians 4:19 (NIV)

So let the image of provision grow in you, and begin to influence your environment.

2. Jehovah Rapha–The Lord our Healer

"I will put none of these diseases upon thee, which I have brought upon the Egyptians: for I am the Lord that healeth thee." Exodus 15:26

Physical healing is a redemptive blessing, paid for on our behalf when Jesus Christ, *"Himself took our infirmities, and bare our sicknesses," (Matthew 8:17b).*

Jesus was whipped, nailed to the cross and humiliated so there could never be any doubt about His will to heal you. His death, burial and resurrection established a covenant of healing with all mankind. He did not only provide healing bread for His children. He did something even greater by becoming our personal Doctor who lives inside us. Child of God, there is a healing Doctor living in you, and He has not lost one case in over two thousand years. Allow this image of the inward Healer to begin growing in your mind's eye until it becomes your inward reality.

I command the healing virtue of Jesus Christ to flow strongly like a river in you now, in Jesus Name!

3. Jehovah Nissi – The Lord our Banner; our Victory

"And the Lord said unto Moses, Write this for a memorial in a book, and rehearse it in the ears of Joshua: for I will utterly put out the remembrance of Amalek from under heaven. And

Moses built an altar, and called the name of it Jehovah-nissi."
Exodus 17:14-15

Jesus' death on the cross secured an eternal victory for every blood-bought Child of God. In my book, *The Cleansing Blood of Christ*, I make mention of this truth, that every time the blood is mentioned, favor and victory are released. Child of God, your Father created you for triumph and victory. Jesus died so you may live. Just like He took our sin and sickness, He also took the sting of shame and defeat. In exchange, He gave us His success.

"Now thanks be unto God, which always causes us to triumph in Christ, and maketh manifest the savour of His knowledge by us in every place." 2 Corinthians 2:14

Say this with me three times, **"I have the Success of Christ!"**

When Jesus arose from the dead, He rose in total victory over every demonic adversary (see *Ephesians 1:20-22*). In addition to Jesus rising from the dead, we also were, *"...risen with Him through the faith of the operation of God, Who hath raised Him from the dead," (Colossians 2:12)*. This is so beautiful; the victory of Christ has become our present inheritance.

"In a loud voice they were saying: Worthy is the Lamb, Who was slain, to receive power and wealth and wisdom and strength and honor and glory and praise!" Revelation 5:12 (NIV).

Yes, this is His inheritance that He is gladly sharing with us!

"And if children, then heirs; heirs of God, and joint-heirs with Christ." Romans 8:17

With this revelation, we as a Church should never bow our knees to the demon of defeat.

Say it with me three times: **"Jesus Christ's success is my present inheritance!"**

4. Jehovah Shalom – The Lord our Peace

"And the Lord said unto him, Peace be unto thee; fear not: thou shalt not die. Then Gideon built an altar there unto the Lord, and called it Jehovah-shalom." Judges 6:23-24

The book of Isaiah, prophesying about Jesus, says that, *"He was wounded for our transgressions, He was bruised for our iniquities: the chastisement of our peace was upon Him; and with His stripes we are healed," (Isaiah 53:5).* Peace is the greatest cry of the human heart. Without it, mankind has no hope. The human soul is like a raging sea without the peace of God. But, thanks be to God, Who has given us His peace in exchange for the war on the inside.

Peace is another redemptive blessing, paid on our behalf and in our name, by Jesus. *Numbers 25:12* says, *"Behold, I give unto him my covenant of peace."*

Jesus strengthened that thought by saying: *"Peace I leave with you, My peace I give unto you: not as the world giveth, give I unto you. Let not your heart be troubled, neither let it be afraid," (John 14:27).*

Benefits of Peace

Peace is a redemptive blessing that was given to us as an inheritance because of Jesus' sufferings at the cross. Out of honor for Him, we should pursue peace with ourselves and all men.

"And, having made peace through the blood of His cross, by Him to reconcile all things unto Himself; by Him, I say, whether they be things in Earth, or things in Heaven." Colossians 1:20

This is so powerful! Jesus made peace with God on our behalf.

A. Peace sets the pace for all divine interventions. If you desire to see God in action, let peace be your guide and friend: *"Be still, and know that I am God: I will be exalted among the heathen, I will be exalted in the earth," (Psalm 46:10).*

B. Peace sets the pace for answered prayer. Paul admonishes us to: *"Be careful for nothing; but in everything by prayer and supplication with thanksgiving, let your requests be made known unto God," (Philippians 4:6).*

"And the God of peace shall bruise satan under your feet shortly." Romans 16:20

C. Peace sets the pace for prosperity. *"Thou wilt keep him in perfect peace, whose mind is stayed on Thee: because he trusteth in Thee. Trust ye in the LORD for ever: for in the LORD JEHOVAH is everlasting strength." Isaiah 26:3-4*

5. Jehovah Raah – The Lord our Shepherd

"The Lord is my shepherd; I shall not want. He maketh me to lie down in green pastures: He leadeth me beside the still waters. He restoreth my soul: He leadeth me in the paths of righteousness for His name's sake." Psalm 23:1-3

To succeed in life, you must be able make the right choices and decisions. Guidance and wisdom are also included in our redemption package.

Jesus Christ became an offering for our sin and shed His blood. He endured punishment for all of mankind, and once the debt was fully paid, our ability to receive divine signals was restored. No longer does satan have the right to confuse and deceive us. His power over us has been broken by the blood of Jesus. Now, we are free to receive clear signals from the Master within.

"And the Lord shall guide thee continually, and satisfy thy soul in drought, and make fat thy bones: and thou shalt be like a watered garden, and like a spring of water, whose waters fail not." Isaiah 58:11

"Thou shalt guide me with Thy counsel." Psalm 73:24

"I will instruct thee and teach thee in the way which thou shalt go: I will guide thee with Mine eye." Psalm 32:8

6. Jehovah Shammah – The Lord is Present

Our divine friendship with God is a very unique redemptive blessing. When man sinned, he lost that friendship and companionship with God. He became one with sin, and satan was his lord and master.

"But God, Who is rich in mercy, for His great love wherewith He loved us, Even when we were dead in sins, hath quickened us together with Christ, (by grace ye are saved;) And hath raised us up together, and made us sit together in heavenly places in Christ Jesus." Ephesians 2:4-6

Now that the debt of sin has been paid, we have been restored to God's presence. We are no longer strangers, but friends. Because we are friends, we can have confidence and boldness in His presence. How sad that most believers are not even aware of these redemptive facts. Their internal world is still governed by fear, sickness and poverty. I declare today, a new generation is coming on the horizon! Refuse to be governed by the seed of negativity. Many still live with a guilty conscience, full of past sins. This is the weapon satan uses most to cripple your faith. Child of God, shake off fear, doubt and lack because provision has been made for these things. The debt has been paid in full. No more payment can be made because that debt no longer exists.

"For this is My blood of the New Testament, which is shed for many for the remission of sins." Matthew 26:28

"Now where remission of these is, there is no more offering for sin." Hebrews 10:18

You are free to enjoy His presence.

7. Jehovah Tsidkenu – God is our Righteousness

"In his days Judah shall be saved, and Israel shall dwell safely: and this is His name whereby He shall be called, The Lord our Righteousness." Jeremiah 23:6

Children of God, because of our loving Savior, all of our past, present and future sins have already been paid for, on our behalf and in our name.

"Who His own self bare our sins in His own body on the tree, that we, being dead to sins, should live unto righteousness: by Whose stripes ye were healed." 1 Peter 2:24

In the Scripture from Jeremiah, we are told that the Lord is our righteousness. How can this be when we have sin in our lives, and have broken the laws of God? Yes, we have sin, and we still do sin, and the wages of sin is still death. But something happened over two thousand years ago that caused the curse of sin to lose its power. This includes our past, present and future sins. They have no power over us, as long as we are conscious of His righteousness. The Bible tells us that, *"God took the sinless Christ and poured into Him our sins. Then, in exchange, He poured God's goodness into us!" (2 Corinthians 5:21, TLB).*

That is why I love the old hymn by Ellis J. Crum, *He Paid a Debt He Did not Owe*.

"He paid a debt He did not owe;

I owed a debt I could not pay;

I needed someone to wash my sins away."

"Being justified freely by His grace through the redemption that is in Christ Jesus: Whom God hath set forth to be a propitiation through faith in His blood, to declare His righteousness for the remission of sins that are past, through the forbearance of God." Romans 3:24-25

"For by a single offering He has forever completely cleansed and perfected those who are consecrated and made holy." Hebrews 10:14 (AMP)

I want you to be very mindful of what the image of God's nature is like. As you begin the process of reprogramming yourself for all of God's best, let the image of His nature grow in you. As I said in the beginning of the chapter, the image you behold, is the image you become!

CHAPTER TWO

THE PAIN OF LACK
AND THE WILL TO WIN

"Poverty and disgrace come to him who ignores instruction, but whoever heeds reproof is honored." Proverbs 13:18 (ESV)

S uccess is the birthright of every child of God. If you are experiencing lack, you will have great difficulties being an effective leader in the 21st century, even though you are a Christian. There is simply no way to achieve your goals, be a blessing to your family, or help the poor if you are broke.

As a young man, I was pained to my core by the knowledge that my father's life was significantly shortened due to lack. I could not take care of him or send him money because I was broke. That is why I have such a passion to teach people how they can receive the blessing of God in their families. I have experienced the frustration of being unable to provide well for my family. As a result, I have developed a stubborn will to win.

I have spent many years studying and applying God's principles of success. As a result, I have come from extreme poverty, to enjoying His abundant provision. I made a vow to take advantage of every opportunity to show others how to gain mastery over lack. We all have a responsibility to take care of those people God places in our lives, and we cannot fulfill this responsibility if we are broke.

This book is not about pleasing religious people. By religious people, I mean people who do not really know God fully. They trust their rules and laws, and they think God is quite mean and carries a big stick. They think He likes us to struggle and be poor. For years, I have tried to persuade religious people that God is for them. Then I discovered that other great men and women of God have also tried this and failed. After following Jesus for over twenty years, I have come to the conclusion that religion is poison; it is toxic to human potential. Let me illustrate how a religious spirit damages people with a story from my own life.

When I was about ten years old, a hurricane roared through my island village in the Caribbean. Many homes were damaged or destroyed. Our garden was also destroyed, and our guinea pigs, goats and sheep were killed. This was very devastating for us, as we depended on all these things for our livelihood. My mother went to the governmental minister responsible for disaster relief, to ask him for some help. This man was also the pastor of a church. He said, "Mrs. Weekes, we cannot help you. We have to look into why this has happened to you. Maybe this is an act of God."

When I heard that, I became very angry with God. I thought, "We are already poor. Why would God come to our village and destroy our things?" So I said to myself, "I will never serve a cruel God like that!"

Religion has been responsible for more pain than joy, and more war than peace. Religion teaches us that we have to be perfect to be saved. My friend, I have found something better than religion. I have found Life in Jesus Christ.

As I examined the life of Jesus, I discovered that He, also, had problems with religious people. They tried to control Him, and when they could not, they committed the ultimate crime and killed Him. Through His death and resurrection, however, His life became a seed from which sprang a new race of Kingdom Builders. God's Kingdom is all about love, hope, joy, life and abundance. I hope you are one of these builders! During my years as a minister, I have been grieved to see what religious people have done to God's children, who are the kings and princes of the earth. In *Revelation 1:6*, Jesus reveals that He has *"... made us kings and priests..."*

Religion turns princes into beggars, and kings into slaves. Nevertheless, God has a plan to bring His people into abundance, prosperity and fulfillment. That is God's plan for YOU, and I believe this is one of the reasons you are now reading this book.

The Will to Win

"Now thanks be unto God, which always causeth us to triumph in Christ, and maketh manifest the savor of His knowledge by us in every place." 2 Corinthians 2:14

Child of God, we are of a different race in Christ Jesus; a race of champions and heroes. Winning in life is our inheritance, and God has infused within our very beings the will to win. The day we were born again, we became part of a winning family. In our family, failure is not an option. We were born into a family of over-comers. Even when it looks like we are losing, we cannot lose. Now is the time for all of us to know our roots, so that we can become fully established. Let me introduce you to your family:

The Spirit of Victory Is in Our Family

"Then went Samson down ...... and, behold, a young lion roared against him. And the Spirit of the LORD came mightily upon him, and he rent him as he would have rent a kid, and he had nothing in his hand." Judges 14:5-6

I see you now ripping in half the spirit of failure that has been harassing your destiny, in Jesus Name!

"These be the names of the mighty men whom David had: ... Adino the Eznite: he lift[ed] up his spear against eight hundred, whom he slew at one time." 2 Samuel 23:8

Did you see that? This same Spirit of Might is in you! He runs in your bloodline! He runs in your family! Glory be to God!

I declare that your confidence is coming back. Your fire is being kindled afresh, now!

"And after him was Eleazar the son of Dodo the Ahohite, one of the three mighty men with David, when they defied the Philistines that were there gathered together to battle; he arose, and smote the Philistines until his hand was weary, and his hand clave unto the sword: and the Lord wrought a great victory that day; and the people returned after him only to spoil." 2 Samuel 23:9-10

I see, by virtue of your family lineage, everything that has been stolen from you is coming back now, in Jesus Name!

"And after him was Shammah the son of Agee the Hararite. And the Philistines were gathered together into a troop, where was a piece of ground full of lentils: and the people fled from the Philistines. But he stood in the midst of the ground, and

defended it, and slew the Philistines: and the Lord wrought a great victory." 2 Samuel 23:11-12

I see you standing and defending everything and everyone the Lord has given you, in Jesus Name! While others are running, you will take your stand!

"And what shall I more say? For the time would fail me to tell of Gideon, and of Barak, and of Samson, and of Jephthae; of David also, and Samuel, and of the prophets: Who through faith subdued kingdoms, wrought righteousness, obtained promises, stopped the mouths of lions, quenched the violence of fire, escaped the edge of the sword, out of weakness were made strong, waxed valiant in fight, turned to flight the armies of the aliens. Women received their dead raised to life again: and others were tortured, not accepting deliverance; that they might obtain a better resurrection." Hebrews 11:32-35

Say this with me three times, **"I was born into a family of champions and I possess the will to win!"**

Child of God, you need to know by revelation that you are different. As a member of God's family, you are called to live each day in victory. This is your redemptive birthright. In this book, I am going to show you how you can reprogram your inner self; both your conscious and subconscious, for success. You will be given keys to help you reprogram your thinking for victory.

I would like you to take a few moments now, to make a list of things that you know are preventing you from being successful. This purpose of this exercise is so that when you have finished implementing the principles in this book, you can look back and see how much ground you have gained. What are some of the things you think may be stopping you from becoming all God wants you to become? I am releasing my faith that you will see how God has already given you keys to overcome these things.

Watch your thoughts, they become words! Watch your words, they become actions! Watch your actions, they become habits! Watch your habits, they become your character! Watch your character, it becomes your destiny–which influences your world!

Be Happy You Are Not of This World

We are living in a world with so much information. Even though we have some great teachers and fine universities and colleges, many people experience very little success. Some reports suggest that only five percent of the entire world's population experience any real form of success. This leaves a shocking ninety-five percent of humanity living mediocre lives, and failing to achieve their dreams. "Why," you ask? The reason for all this personal defeat is very simple.

Knowledge Does not Change You, Habit Does

Please do not misunderstand me, knowledge is powerful. But until knowledge becomes your habitual inner mindset, no changes will take place. I have met many good people who claim to know everything, yet what they claim to know has not changed them. Until new knowledge becomes an habitual mindset, that knowledge will be just like a warm bath. It will cool down and dissipate with time.

Spell of Failure

I hate the thought of failing, and I am sure you do too. Sometimes we fail because we lack maturity or skills. These types of setbacks, if we have the right attitude, can become stepping stones to something great. There is something that I call the spell of failure which manifests in a life that has been programmed for mediocrity. As a child, I saw this first hand with many of my childhood friends. Like them, I had no motivation to excel. I had suffered so much inner bruising and rejection that I was afraid to even try.

The Word of God teaches us that, *"The thief cometh not, but for to steal, and to kill, and to destroy: I am come that they might have life, and that they might have it more abundantly," (John 10:10)*. Can we have abundant life in this world? Emphatically, yes! Abundant life is possible–because of our wonderful Jesus! He is the best thing that ever happened to me. He is the foundation of all human dignity. I only wish the church would preach this message even more.

So how does this relate to reprogramming ourselves for success? First of all, we need to realize that the opposite of success is failure, and failure is a spirit. We are dealing with a spirit here. The principles and teachings in this book aim to reprogram and fine tune your subconscious mind, so that the atmosphere around you will be saturated with success. Just like Jesus was wired to succeed, you also are wired for success. He had a will to win. He was completely synchronized with His identity and the victorious ways of His Father. Because of that, He was able to live a life filled with miracles and exploits. Jesus has redeemed you from mediocrity, and as you synchronize your mind to His Word, you, too, are destined for exploits!

Standing Against satan's Lies

"For we wrestle not against flesh and blood, but against principalities, against powers, against the rulers of the darkness of this world, against spiritual wickedness in high places."
Ephesians 6:12

The only weapons satan has to use against believers are lies and deception. These tricks have no real power because he himself has no authentic power. The Word of God tells us that Jesus has all the power. Since Jesus has all the power, of course satan has none! The devil will not just give up though. Sometimes you need to tell him to shut up! Otherwise, he will try everything possible to keep you focused on the natural realm of the five senses. Your job is to remain in the Spirit, and stay connected by faith to the Word. If you do these things, you will be victorious.

Guard Your Mind

"Keep thy heart with all diligence; for out of it are the issues of life." Proverbs 4:23

The New English Bible translation of this verse says, *"Guard your heart with all vigilance, for from it are the sources of life."*

In *1 Peter 1:13 (ESV),* Peter teaches: *"Therefore, preparing your minds for action, and being sober-minded, set your hope fully on the grace that will be brought to you at the revelation of Jesus Christ."*

Your mind is a crucial asset to living a victorious life. Good and evil battle for your mind, and whichever one captures your mind wins your soul. The mind is the eye of a person. Whatever you envision and accept in your mind is what you use to influence and shape your world. The devil puts pressure on your mind and body to try and convince you that God does not really mean what He said. The devil does not want you to influence anyone or anything for good. The great news is, he will never succeed in defeating anyone whose mind is stayed consistently on God. As long as you guard your mind, the enemy cannot touch you! If, however, you allow him to capture your mind, you become his slave. *Romans 8:6 says, "For to be carnally*

minded is death; but to be spiritually minded is life and peace."
A carnal mind is a dark mind filled with fear and worry, and
polluted with unclean thoughts. A carnal mind is opposed to
the ways of God. The Word tells us that, *"...the mind of the
flesh [with its carnal thoughts and purposes] is hostile to God,
for it does not submit itself to God's Law; indeed it cannot. So
then those who are living the life of the flesh [catering to the
appetites and impulses of their carnal nature] cannot please or
satisfy God, or be acceptable to Him," (Romans 8:7-8, AMP).*

The devil will use the thoughts of a carnal person to hold
that person in captivity. However, the spiritual mind is a friend
of God, free from fear and full of peace. It is renewed to think
like God. Let us look at some of the benefits we will enjoy when
our mind is renewed by the Word of God.

Ten Benefits of a Spirit Led Mind

**1. You will come to know the will of God, which is good, per-
fect and acceptable**. *"And be not conformed to this world: but
be ye transformed by the renewing of your mind, that ye may
prove what is that good, and acceptable, and perfect, will of
God." Romans 12:2*

2. You will have peace. *"You will guard him and keep him in
perfect and constant peace whose mind [both its inclination
and its character] is stayed on You, because he commits himself to You, leans on You, and hopes confidently in You." Isaiah
26:3 (AMP)*

**3. You will live in right relationship with God and have no
condemnation.** *"Strip yourselves of your former nature [put off
and discard your old unrenewed self] which characterized your
previous manner of life and becomes corrupt through lusts and
desires that spring from delusion; and be constantly renewed*

46

in the spirit of your mind [having a fresh mental and spiritual attitude]." Ephesians 4:22-23 (AMP)

4. You will live in holiness. *"And put on the new nature (the regenerate self) created in God's image, [Godlike] in true righteousness and holiness." Ephesians 4:24 (AMP)*

5. You will live in divine health. *"Beloved, I pray that you may prosper in every way and [that your body] may keep well, even as [I know] your soul keeps well and prospers." 3 John 1:2 (AMP)*

6. You will be free from all bondage. *"So Jesus said to those Jews who had believed in Him, if you abide in My Word [hold fast to My teachings and live in accordance with them], you are truly My disciples. And you will know the Truth, and the Truth will set you free." John 8:31-32 (AMP)*

7. You will experience financial freedom. *"And the Lord shall make you have a surplus of prosperity, through the fruit of your body, of your livestock, and of your ground, in the land which the Lord swore to your fathers to give you." Deuteronomy 28:11 (AMP)*

8. You will project confidence and boldness. *"I have strength for all things in Christ who empowers me [I am ready for anything and equal to anything through Him who infuses inner strength into me; I am self-sufficient in Christ's sufficiency]." Philippians 4:13 (AMP)*

9. You will have a positive attitude and be very optimistic toward life. *"Be anxious for nothing, but in everything by prayer and supplication, with thanksgiving, let your requests be made known to God; and the peace of God, which surpasses* *all understanding, will guard your hearts and minds through Christ Jesus." Philippians 4:6-7 (NKJV)*

10. You will be clear, sharp, focused and alert. *"Where there is no revelation, the people cast off restraint; But happy is he who keeps the law." Proverbs 29:18 (NKJV)*

CHAPTER THREE

CONQUERING THE SPIRIT OF FAILURE

"**Y**ou may encounter many defeats, but you must not be defeated. In fact, it may be necessary to encounter the defeats, so you can know who you are, what you can rise from, and how you can still come out of it."

— Maya Angelou

"For whatsoever is born of God overcometh the world: and this is the victory that overcometh the world, even our faith."
1 John 5:4

There is a big difference between failure and failing. Failure is a spirit that is assigned to cripple your God-given potential. When a person has many negative life experiences, they may come to accept failure as their reality. Failure has no reality; it has no home, so it looks for a resting place. Just because someone fails at something does not make them a failure. Failing is actually a part of success, functioning as an indicator when someone misses the mark. Failure is a mindset. You are the only one who can decide whether you are a failure are not. Such a decision cannot be made by your friends, your teachers, your enemies, or even the devil. You only become a failure when you surrender to the emotional weakness of failing. This happens when you accept disappointment, and make it your living and breathing reality.

Avoiding the Failure Company

Failure is a lying spirit, accompanied by many cousins. Therefore, it must be promptly dealt with before it can destroy its victims. The spirit of failure is assigned to extinguish your confidence and hijack your purpose in God. Learn to recognize when failure shows up, knocking at your door disguised as false humility, low self-esteem, fear, pride or shame. All these negative emotions are from the same weak family called failure.

The Bible says, *"Cast not away therefore your confidence, which hath great recompense of reward," (Hebrews 10:35)*. God uses your confidence in Him to bring rewards to you. These rewards are associated with success. Sometimes, people in the world tend to have a better perspective on winning than most Christians. The world has rejected the Lordship of Jesus. Sadly though, while the church has been praying for increase, the world has accepted His principles of success and gone on to make millions.

Using Failure as Motivation

My friend, you do not need to fear failure, since Jesus has already defeated it. By refusing to focus on failure, you successfully dis-empower it. Do not waste time fighting the darkness! Just let your light shine, and you will see your way to good success.

Throughout history, men and women with lesser abilities than you and I have become great. Their secret? They refused to see themselves as failures. This mindset was their pathway to greatness.

Henry Ford had only six months of formal education when he began his career as a bicycle mechanic. He failed over and over again. Henry was broke seven times, but he refused to see himself as a failure. At the time of his death, he was listed as one of the top ten wealthiest people of all times, and now has a net worth of $200 Billion, (http://www.celebritynetworth.com/richest-businessmen/ceos/henry-ford-net-worth/).

The parents of Albert Einstein thought he was mentally disturbed because he did not talk until he was three years old. (Some folks thought he was simply waiting until he had something worthwhile to say!) I hope you understand what I am trying to say. Failure is a spirit that will keep knocking on the doors of every great leader. If you do not conquer this spirit, it will keep on knocking. Every great leader has failed. However, their secret is that they refused to see themselves as failures.

Thomas Edison's teacher told his mother that her eleven year old son was,"Too dumb to learn." Evidently, they forgot to tell Edison, because the contributions his inventions made to society testify of his genius. His teachers also believed he was hyperactive, that his brains were addled, and that he was too confused mentally to function properly. If modern psychology had existed when he was a child, young Thomas would likely have been labeled with Attention Deficit Hyperactivity Disorder. Thomas Edison and many of his peers fought against this spirit of failure all their lives. However, they overcame and won! Child of God, always remember that unless this spirit is conquered, it will conquer you.

All great leaders fail, but what sets them apart is they use setbacks to further motivate themselves, and convert their pain into fresh courage. I like what Michael Jordan says concerning failure:

"I've missed more than nine thousand shots in my career. I've lost almost three hundred games. Twenty-six times, I've been trusted to take the game winning shot and missed. I've failed over and over and over again in my life. And that is why I succeed!"

See Yourself the Way God Sees You

When God looks at you, He sees a winner! He wants you to see yourself as a winner also, and as His highest creation. The internal picture you develop of yourself is critical to your failure or success. When you see yourself with the mind of Christ, you will see yourself as a portrait of success. Now that you are born again, you are not the same person you once were. Your nature, as a son or daughter of God, is the nature of success. Did you know that God has a marvelous photo album filled with a trillion perfect pictures of you? He sees all your high-points, good qualities, and positive attributes. The devil always tries to show photos of you at your worst and remind you of what you were like at your weakest point. Do yourself a favor and do not believe him. The devil is the father of all lies and cannot see your destiny or your greatness, because they are in Christ.

From Dunce to Genius

Years ago, I read about a British genius who was told as a youth that he was a dunce. When Victor Serebriakoff was fifteen years old, he was written off as an underachiever. His teacher told him he would never be able to finish school and advised him to drop out and learn a trade. Victor took that counsel, and for the next seventeen years was an itinerant worker. Since he was told he was a dunce, he acted like one for seventeen years. When he was thirty-two years old however, Victor was evaluated and his I.Q. registered an amazing one hundred sixty-one, ranking him as a genius! Victor's image of himself immediately transformed and he began to act like the genius he was. Since that time, he has written books, produced a number of patents, and become a successful businessman. One of the crowning achievements of this high school dropout was his election to Chairman of the *International Mensa Society*. The Mensa Society has only one membership qualification: a minimum I.Q. of one hundred-forty.

No More Excuses–Your Time Has Come

Here are some questions for you to ask yourself. Do you know who you are? Have you ever answered that question? Have you just settled and accepted the weak opinions of others, rather than what God has to say concerning you? Your birth was not an accident. You are here in answer to the deep cries of those who have gone before you. This is your time and moment to manifest the greatness of your true nature. Refuse to accept small or negative opinions that others may have about you. Now, are you ready to dig deep into your soul to find the treasures and gold within?

It is time for the real you to stand up! Not the person who always makes excuses. Not the old you, who has been programmed negatively by others. The you God sees every day needs to arise; the champion you of whom all hell is afraid of, because they see you in Christ. That is the person who needs to stand up. It is time for you to stand tall and see your dreams realized! It is time for you to complete that course, start that business, and get into shape! It is time to let go of whatever holds you back and rise above average thinking! Lastly, it is time to break off the sabotaging mindset that has held you captive! My friend, it is your time to fly! Do not be afraid any longer! I am not here to condemn you, but to inspire you to be your best. We all blossom in the things we enjoy, which come naturally to us. However, now is the time to advance to a new level of greatness. I encourage you to challenge yourself and break free from mediocrity, starting this very day!

Paying the Price for Success

Success comes with a price tag attached, labeled: *hard work.* You have to pay first, before you can enjoy! Muhammad Ali once said, "If success was easy, everybody would do it." He also said, "I hated every minute of training, but I said, Don't quit. Suffer now and live the rest of your life as a champion."

Michael Jordan woke up at five a.m. to work on his jump shot. He frequently practiced for seven or eight hours a day. What these men were doing was paying the price for their dreams. Nothing is as easy as it looks at the start. Nothing worthwhile is simple. Every great accomplishment is the result of hundreds and thousands of small efforts that no one can see or appreciate. Great success is the result of many years of hard work. Nothing great comes easy. Occasionally, you may read in the newspaper about people who have become successful overnight. My friend, that is not the norm. Therefore, do not become discouraged if this is not your case. Just keep working on your dreams. Sometimes you will have to burn the midnight oil and go without sleep, but do it anyway!

Success demands we change. We must turn fear into courage, pain into motivation, and weakness into strength. Success will not negotiate with failure, but always presses toward the greater life. I often say that until you have failed ten thousand times, like Thomas Edison, you are not qualified to quit. So keep working on yourself and your dreams, until things begin to get better.

"Move out of your comfort zone. You can only grow if you are feeling awkward and uncomfortable when you are trying something new. If it does not challenge you, it does not change you." Brian Tracy

Comfort is one of the biggest enemies of achievement. Never retire, just get re-fired. Until all your dreams come to pass, keep pressing forward. It is never too late.

It took me almost twenty years to finally get my driver's license. Can you imagine that? I had managed to conquer so many weaknesses in my life, but this one area was a big one. I just became so comfortable having people drive me. One day, I got so tired of having my wife and friends drive me that it made me sick! All I can say is something snapped inside. One day I screamed at the top of my voice, "Enough is enough–this is not Kingdom living!" My entire freedom was at the mercy of others. I was not born to beg; I am a child of the King. As a result, that summer I took professional driving lessons. Today I have my license, and I love the freedom that driving has given me! Someone once said that pain can be the greatest motivator, and I cannot agree more!

CHAPTER FOUR

THE ANOINTING FOR SUCCESS

"Thus says the Lord, your Redeemer, the Holy One of Israel. "I am the Lord your God, Who teaches you to profit, Who leads you in the way you should go." Isaiah 48:17 (NKJV)

There is such a thing called the anointing for success. The anointing for success gives you ability to do things without struggle and frustration. Success is your birthright. You have a covenant right to succeed. An eagle is programmed to fly, fish are programmed to swim, and you my friend, have a blood-bought right to succeed. Our Scripture above gives us powerful insight regarding our covenant of success.

Child of God, one thing you need to understand is that God is committed to your rising. He has promised to lead and guide you into the realm of profit. This is so contrary to what religion has taught us. Religion wants us to struggle, but God wants us to profit.

Another Scripture I love is from *2 Chronicles 26:5*. It says, *"As long as [Uzziah] sought the Lord, God made him to prosper."* Did you hear that? As long as you and I keep our eyes on God and His Word, He will cause us to prosper. In other words, if you keep your eyes on Jesus, He will turn you into a bundle of success. I love that!

Developing an Attitude for Success

I like the word attitude because it speaks of your mood, or your mental state. Your attitude determines your altitude, or how far and high you go in life. So what is your attitude for success? What are your thoughts about winning? My friend, winning is a spirit, and all about your attitude. Do you know that God wants you to win all the time? Do you have this mindset? It is important to develop the right attitude for success, and this begins with the will to win.

"So David waxed greater and greater: for the Lord of hosts was with him." 1 Chronicles 11:9

My friend, do you have a dream to win in life? Do you have a dream to excel and obtain all that God has for you? The good news is that this is exactly God's plan. His dream for you is that you constantly make progress. God is not satisfied with where you are at this moment. He wants you to experience success after success. This is what Jesus meant when He was teaching His disciples in *John 15:1-8*.

So develop an attitude for success. Become conscious of success, and it will follow you. Success encompasses how you think, the words you speak, and the people you influence. God has more for you!

Do you know that both poverty and riches are the offspring of a person's thinking? You are programmed with thoughts of either poverty or increase, sickness or health. The good news is, you can choose to reprogram yourself with new thoughts of success.

Child of God, God has increase on His mind for you. (See *Psalm 115:14* and *Colossians 2:19*.) The question is: do you have increase on your mind? Do you have thoughts of increase in your imagination? This is so important because whatever you have in your thoughts will enter into your life. The thoughts that are ingrained in you control your life. They determine who you will meet, and where you want to go in life. They even determine who you will marry. Yes, they do.

I like something that Napoleon Hill said, "When thinking is mixed with feelings and emotions, a magnetic force field forms that will attract similar or related thoughts and experiences." In other words, your brain is not just a computer that stores information. Your brain is a magnet and will attract thoughts based on how it has been empowered. Your mind has the power within itself to create shortage, lack scarcity. On the contrary, if it is programmed with success, love, prosperity, promotion, and abundance, nothing can stop you from becoming a success.

To help people with this, in our *School of the Supernatural*, I designed a course specifically addressing these concepts. In the class, I talk about the importance of developing an atmosphere for success. You have to talk and think success in order to be programmed with, and experience it. This is because success only comes to those who are aware of it. Therefore, anchor your soul to success.

The Covenant of Success

"Christ hath redeemed us from the curse of the law, being made a curse for us: for it is written, Cursed is every one that hangeth on a tree: That the blessing of Abraham might come on the Gentiles through Jesus Christ; that we might receive the promise of the Spirit through faith." Galatians 3:13-14

In the Kingdom of God, success and victory are your birthright. Everything that pertains to life and godliness have been paid for you by the death, burial, and resurrection of Jesus. Child of God, success is a covenant, paid for us by the blood of Jesus. We just need to place a demand on it.

"But Christ being come an High Priest of good things to come, by a greater and more perfect tabernacle, not made with hands, that is to say, not of this building; Neither by the blood of goats and calves, but by His own blood He entered in once into the holy place, having obtained eternal redemption for us. For if the blood of bulls and of goats, and the ashes of an heifer sprinkling the unclean, sanctifieth to the purifying of the flesh: How much more shall the blood of Christ, who through the eternal Spirit offered Himself without spot to God, purge your conscience from dead works to serve the living God?" Hebrews 9:11-14

You must know the price Jesus paid for your success! Because He paid the ultimate price, your success is in God, and part of your covenant with Him. Jesus' blood is what guarantees your success. Not the blood of bulls and goats, but by Jesus' very blood, which He freely and willingly offered Himself: *"For this is My blood of the New Testament, which is shed for many for the remission of sins,"* (Matthew 26:28).

Child of God, your success and victory in Christ are non-negotiable. They are not up for discussion or debate. They are part of your covenant! The Holy Spirit will fiercely judge the individual or system that dares to break the seal of this vow because the Scriptures cannot be broken. Now, since our success and greatness were sealed in blood, we, as children of God, should have steadfast confidence about winning in life.

Throughout the Bible, we see the weak, the strong, kings, and even slaves, express enormous faith in God. As a result, they win! When I think of the power that was working in the lives of

Abraham, Moses, David, Solomon and many others, I realize their victories and successes were rooted in the blood covenant.

What Is a Covenant?

A covenant is more than a promise, but is made up of many promises. In every covenant, blood must be shed. It must cost you something to make a covenant. Let me explain. When God made a promise to Abram (*Genesis 12:1-7*), it was just a promise. However, Abram acted in faith and circumcised himself and his household, the promise graduated into a covenant. (See *Genesis 17:11-27*).

I like Bishop David Oyedepo's definition of a covenant. He says, "A covenant is like a contract. It involves two or more people. In this case, it involves just you and God. God is the *Covenantor* or guarantor and you become the *covenantee*, or the beneficiary of the deal. The covenant is not like a promise. It is a vow that cannot be broken once the required conditions have been met." Wow! That is good! Hear what God says about His Word: *"My covenant will I not break, nor alter the thing that is gone out of My lips," (Psalm 89:34).*

In my church I explain covenant this way: "When you meet the demands of Scripture by acting in faith and totally relying on God's grace, your actions are interpreted as a covenant."

Another verse that illustrates this is *Psalm 50:5*. God says to, *"Gather my saints together unto Me, those that have made a covenant with Me by sacrifice."* When we give to God sacrificially, our giving becomes a covenant. God is then committed to our actions, like He is committed to all other covenant actions.

Secret Keys to Success

"And the Lord was with Joseph, and he was a prosperous man; and he was in the house of his master the Egyptian. And his master saw that the Lord was with him, and that the Lord made all that he did to prosper in his hand." Genesis 39:2-3

God's definition of success is contrary to that of the world. The world's definition is based on possessions and accomplishments, but no amount of these things can truly measure success. Rather, success is a spirit that drives you to become everything God has called you to be. I call it: the indwelling Presence of God that leads you to victory.

Joseph was sold into slavery in Egypt as a young boy. He went there with nothing. No contacts, no educational qualifications, and no cultural connections. Even the precious gift from his father, the splendid coat of many colors, was taken from him. He had nothing! He was sold as a naked slave, yet the Bible says he was a success, because the Lord was with him. In the above Scripture, we can see very clearly that Joseph's life exemplified this truth. Success is not what you have, but Whose you are, and Who is with you.

Inspirational Success

There are several other ways success is measured by. Some of them are: your ways of thinking, the ideas you possess, the things you do, and the words that come out of your mouth. Moreover, success also causes you to influence those around you to think like you. I remember being so influenced by Martin Luther King Jr. as a child. He changed the world with his words, his love and his convictions about equality. A more modern example is President Obama; not Obama the politician, but Obama the inspiration. You and I may not like some things about the president, but the purpose of my book is not to be political. I will leave that to the politicians and critics. My book is to convey a story of success and hope.

This man was raised by a single mother without a father, in the middle of poverty and psychological hardship. Nevertheless, he rose above all that to become the ~~leader of the free world~~ *President*. I know there is hope for every single mother who is raising her child alone. Because of Barak Obama's life, millions of people now believe their dreams are possible. That, my friend, is a success story, and inspiration for all of us.

In 2009, I took a team of leaders from my church, along with my wife and our four children to the Caribbean where I was born and raised. I wanted them to see where God had brought their pastor/husband/dad from. This trip was a very emotional one for me. We paid visits to several places, but the one that touched me the most was my old high school. This was where I had been told that I would never amount to anything good in life. As I walked through the classrooms and talked with some of the teachers, I saw a large picture of President Obama on the wall. Underneath was a caption that said, "If you can dream it, you can have it." I wept when I saw that, because the room that had been my place of pain, had now become a place of dreams and inspiration for every young boy and girl in my village.

Contending for Success

"Teach those who are rich in this world not to be proud and not to trust in their money, which is so unreliable. Their trust should be in God, who richly gives us all we need for our enjoyment."
1 Timothy 6:17 (NLT)

Did you see that? All things are yours to enjoy in Christ! Refuse to settle for a lower life than what Christ has made available to you. Poverty, sickness, and defeat are not yours. They are contrary to the life of blessing. Make up your mind, child of God, to live triumphantly every day. This is the will of God for you.

Jesus suffered on the cross to give you a life of blessing. Blessings will not manifest in your life automatically though, there will be a fight. The little devil, who has already been defeated, will still try to convince you that you lack the qualifications to walk in God's best. Your inheritance, which is in the world of the Spirit, belongs to you, but you will need to contend in order to possess it.

Many believers have failed at this level of warfare. Many are afraid to even use the Word as a weapon. Think about it. If there was no opposition, your inheritance would have been automatically released to you. There is indeed opposition, so wake up and contend for what the Lord has given you.

"Rise ye up, take your journey, and pass over the river Arnon: behold, I have given into thine hand Sihon the Amorite, king of Heshbon, and his land: begin to possess it, and contend with him in battle. This day will I begin to put the dread of thee and the fear of thee upon the nations that are under the whole heaven, who shall hear report of thee, and shall tremble, and be in anguish because of thee." Deuteronomy 2:24-25

God also told us in the book of *Nehemiah 4:14*, "*And I looked, and rose up, and said unto the nobles, and to the rulers, and to the rest of the people, Be not ye afraid of them: remember the Lord, which is great and terrible, and fight for your brethren, your sons, and your daughters, your wives, and your houses.*"

If we fail to contend, we will never lay hold of our inheritance. We will be victims in life, and this is not our portion.

Remember, in our Kingdom, we do not fight for victory. We contend from a place of victory. We have the victory, but it needs to be enforced, because the devil is a thieving outlaw. Jesus has deposited our victory into our accounts. The cheque is yours, you just need to cash it.

"Now thanks be unto God, which always causeth us to triumph in Christ, and maketh manifest the savour of His knowledge by us in every place." 2 Corinthians 2:14

How Do We Fight?

Let's say you are believing God for healing in your body, or for a financial need. When you check your bank account, it appears you will not be able to meet your commitments. Right away, satan attacks your mind with thoughts of lack and insufficiency. He keeps reminding you that you will never get out of this situation, and the cycle of lack will never be broken. How, you ask, should you respond to these weak thoughts? I'm glad you asked! This type of situation is what Dr. T.L. Osborn defines as truth being on trial. Life challenges and difficult situations are testing the Word of God you say you believe. The good news is that it is an open book test! All the answers to the test are in the Book and you always win! Sadly, many of God's precious people are not aware of this, so they become victims of life circumstances.

My friend, in every test there are always three witnesses. They are God's Word, the problem, and you. Please listen to me carefully here. At this level of warfare, you are the established witness! You determine what will happen to your finances, and to your life. It is not God, and definitely not satan. You have to settle in your heart of hearts that you are completely one with God, and fight from a standpoint of victory. Remind the devil, and all apparent contrary evidence, that you are not poor, trying to be rich, or sick trying to be healed. My friend, you are whole in Christ, and that is your rich inheritance. One of satan's biggest strategies is to make you think you do not have what you already have in Christ. By trying to convince you that God does not mean what He says, satan hopes to cheat you out of your inheritance. He uses the same old lie over and over again. Sadly, many have taken his bait. They begin to doubt God and cannot receive anything from Him. This deceptive scheme of satan's must be exposed with the light of God's Word.

Child of God, you have to win at this level of warfare. The war is all in your mind. Consequently, if you win in the mind, you will win in the natural. Your mind is the highest level where warfare is fought. That is why satan is after it. Protect your mind, for it will either bring you victory, or become the groundwork for failure. The choice is yours. The Bible says, *"I have set before you life and death,....choose life, that...you... may live," (Deuteronomy 30:19 NKJV).* Beloved, I also urge you to choose life!

CHAPTER FIVE

THE ATMOSPHERE OF SUCCESS

My great mentor Bishop Oyedepo once said, "Every living thing needs an atmosphere conducive for development." The same could be said of success. Your heart is the ground where success grows, and from where it flows. In *Proverbs 4:23 (AMP)* the instruction is to, *"Keep and guard your heart with all vigilance and above all that you guard, for out of it flow the springs of life."*

I have met many people who are looking for success in the wrong places. Some have the erroneous idea that success comes from who you know. Yes, people are important, and they will play a great part in your success story, but please do not be deceived. Success ultimately flows from your heart, not from your connections. The Bible tells us that God has set eternity in your heart, *(Ecclesiastes 3:11)*. Nothing happens by accident to a child of destiny. Everyone who will be an asset to your destiny is already within you in seed form. When your heart attitude is positive and cultured for success, the seed will germinate and you will meet the right people.

Look at this striking example in *Genesis 39:1-3, "And Joseph was brought down to Egypt; and Potiphar, an officer of Pharaoh, captain of the guard, an Egyptian, bought him of the hands of the Ishmaelites, which had brought him down thither. And the Lord was with Joseph, and he was a prosperous man; and he was in the house of his master the Egyptian. And his master saw that the Lord was with him, and that the Lord made all that he did to prosper in his hand."*

The Scripture goes on to tell us that Joseph found grace in Potiphar's sight, and he served him. The question is, why did Potiphar like Joseph? He had nothing! He was sold as a naked slave. He had no point of reference. Let me give you a golden seed. Potiphar liked Joseph because even though he was his master, he was under the influence of Joseph's heart. Never forget that!

Your heart is a miracle incubating center where you conceptualize your destiny and then release it into the earth. Your heart is also a storehouse for divine things. Everything you need to live a victorious life is packaged in your heart. No wonder God wants us to guard and protect our hearts!

Only You Can Stop You

Child of God, the difficult atmosphere around you does not matter. If you have success in your heart, you cannot be stopped! This is why no demonic powers, groups of people, or religious leaders could stop Jesus. *Hebrews 12:2* says that Jesus, *"...for the joy that was set before Him endured the cross."*

Jesus was programmed for success. That is the reason He was able to defeat all His enemies. If we desire to win in life, we also need to be reprogrammed for success.

Your success in every area of life is directly linked to the prosperity contained inside you. Success is found in the prosperity of your soul. There are five things that constitute the soul: the mind, will, imagination, intellect and emotions. To be a success, you need to grow in these five areas.

When I was in the nation of India, my team and I saw a blacksmith making knives and swords. First, he placed a piece of metal in the fire until it became molten hot. Then, holding the glowing red metal with tongs, he struck it over and over with a heavy hammer. Such a clanging rang through the air! As we watched, we suddenly began to see the blade of a sword emerge. I was asked if I wanted to try. As I pounded and perspired, I realized that just hitting that piece of metal with a hammer wasn't enough. I had to see the metal turning into what I wanted to create in my mind's eye. And that is how you incubate success. You have to first see your dream or vision coming to pass internally. Then, with hard work and discipline, you transfer that image into reality.

I shared at the beginning of this chapter the importance of atmosphere. Every plant needs the right conditions to grow. If we desire to see good results or reap a wonderful harvest, we need to foster an atmosphere for success. The first atmospheric factor for success is:

The Law of Growth

The *law of growth* is a vital part of Kingdom success. You should never come to a point in your walk as a believer, or even as a human being, where you stop growing. The day you stop growing is the day you start dying. I once heard a man say, "If your circumstances are bigger than your drive, you will never make it." For this reason, praying in the Spirit is very important, as that is what builds up and vitalizes your inner man. (See *Jude 1:20*).

One young man, at the age of seven, vowed that he would bring his mother and grandmother out of poverty. By the age of thirteen, he had made his first million dollars. He said, "Comfort is the enemy of achievement."

Think about that. I am convinced that if you stick with me through this whole process, you will be able to catch what the Spirit of God is saying in this book, and your life will never be the same. You will become like cold water in a hot desert. Men will run to get to you, in order to drink from the water that is in your well. The world is thirsty and they are looking for leadership. Keep growing, and keep searching, because your finest hour is at hand!

The Law of Meditation and Visualization

Success on the outside is created
by success on the inside!

There are laws in this universe, such as the *law of gravity*, which God has set in place. The *law of cause and effect*, the *law of motion* and the *law of sowing and reaping* were all instated by Him. In the *School of Success*, the *laws of meditation and visualization* are as important as the *law of gravity*. I want you to have as much faith in these principles as you do in the *law of gravity*. The *laws of meditation and visualization* say that whatever you conceive in your heart, you will give birth to without pressure. The whole universe will move out of the way for the image that is in your heart to come forth.

Even God said that He could not stop a group of people from doing what they had imagined in their hearts.

"And the Lord said, Behold, the people is one, and they have all one language; and this they begin to do: and now nothing will be restrained from them, which they have imagined to do."
Genesis 11:6

God knew the people had tapped into the laws we just mentioned.

When your heart is filled with images, they will manifest without you having to do anything. Your job is to put the right images inside, and then the reprogramming of your heart will birth those dreams. Nothing in this universe can stand in the way. The church, over the years, has abandoned these principles. You do not need to pray for things God has already given you. Rather, you need to pray for revelation and insight.

Apostle Charles Ndifon taught me that if you are doing something and it is not working, there is a possibility you are doing something wrong! That is why if things in my life are going wrong, I stop and get on my knees. I ask God to show me what is happening. He will tell me to either keep doing what I am doing, or show me the changes I need to make.

The laws work, and even when one law supersedes another, the superseding law must continually be applied. For example, the *laws of thrust and lift* supersede the *law of gravity*. If this were not true, airplanes would not be able to stay in the air. The minute *thrust and lift* cease to be applied, *gravity* would once again take over and the airplane would plummet to the ground. We have an advantage because we know the laws and we know the Person who made them. He is our Father! How can we fail?

Joshua 1:8 tells how the laws of visualization and meditation will work for you. Read and meditate on Scriptures like this, because you need to get them inside of you. These are laws that govern success, and even if you do not believe in them, they still work!

"This book...shall not depart out of thy mouth; but thou shalt meditate therein day and night, that thou mayest observe to do according to all that is written therein: for then thou shalt make thy way prosperous, and then thou shalt have good success." Joshua 1:8

You shall make your own way prosperous! You do it! God will not do it for you.

"This Book of the Law shall not depart out of your mouth, but you shall meditate on it day and night, that you may observe and do according to all that is written in it. For then you shall make your way prosperous, and then you shall deal wisely and have good success." Joshua 1:8 (AMP)

God wants you to visualize your success until it becomes substance. You need to turn the Scriptures into pictures. Dream and envision the pictures until they become your reality through the power of your renewed mind.

I did not always know these laws. For years I suffered unnecessarily, but the day God opened my mind to these powerful *laws of meditation and visualization*, everything changed. Please do not misunderstand me, I do not live in a perfect world. I just know now what to do, to bring about my desired changes.

Your Outer World is a Reflection of Your Inner World

God's thoughts are full of success, energy and possibility. As you meditate on them, they become grafted into your personality, and then into your life. My friend, if you are really serious about your progress, you need to spend at least ten or fifteen minutes every day visualizing and meditating on your goals and dreams. As you are faithful to do this, every dream and vision in your heart will become a part of you.

Many times, our hearts and minds are already programmed with seeds of failure. As you meditate on your goals and dreams using the *principles of success*, the pain and stain of past failures will be removed. Until you actually do this, you will never manifest your true son-ship.

"Having therefore these promises, dearly beloved, let us cleanse ourselves from all filthiness of the flesh and spirit, perfecting holiness in the fear of God." 2 Corinthians 7:1

I am aware that some people might think this sounds like new age, therefore I will take some time to clearly explain the principles so these powerful truths can be received without offense.

Visualization and meditation are two of the most powerful laws in the *School of Success*. Some people become very uncomfortable with even the mention of these two words, which is very sad. Should we stop meditating because some *new age* guru hums and meditates? Should we go back to riding horses as a means of transportation because the *new age* folks use cars? Should we use steamboats and ships now for our long distance travels because worldly people use airplanes? What has happened to us? Why are we are so afraid? This thinking is so archaic, it will lead us back into the dark ages if we do not change by acquiring knowledge. Now having said all of this, I need to strongly point out, there is a big difference between Biblical meditation and *new age* krishna style meditation, which is counterfeit and very satanic.

New age defines meditation as the practice of training one's mind to drop everything and arrive at a state where only consciousness remains. They tell us to clear the mind and come to a state of emptiness. This exercise is very dangerous and can lead to satanic encounters and mental harassment. In Biblical meditation we fill our minds with God's thoughts and promises. As we practice Kingdom meditation, we turn Scripture into pictures. We see the possibilities of God working in us. *Meditation* also means:

- to center our minds on God's Word
- to ponder, dwell on, consider and contemplate

- to imagine and visualize, think on, and revolve in the mind
- to mutter and speak positively under our breath
- to fix and focus our attention on God's promises, not on life's problems

Looking at this definition, we can see there is a big difference between Biblical meditation and what the world calls meditation. God does not want our minds to be empty, but filled with all of His good promises. King David had this to say about meditation: *"My meditation of Him shall be sweet: I will be glad in the Lord,"* (Psalm 104:34).

"Oh how love I Thy law; it is my meditation all the day... I have more understanding than all my teachers: for Thy testimonies are my meditation." Psalm 119:97, 99

Ten Supernatural Results of Meditation

"Finally, brethren, whatever things are true, whatever things are noble, whatever things are just, whatever things are pure, whatever things are lovely, whatever things are of good report, if there is any virtue and if there is anything praiseworthy—meditate on these things. The things which you learned and received and heard and saw in me, these do, and the God of peace will be with you." Philippians 4:8-9 (NKJV)

Meditating on God and His Word daily will produce at least ten supernatural results. Godly meditation will:

1. Bring us uncommon blessing.

"Blessed is the man that walketh not in the counsel of the ungodly, nor standeth in the way of sinners, nor sitteth in the seat of the scornful. But his delight is in the law of the Lord; and in His law doth he meditate day and night. And he shall be like a tree

planted by the rivers of water, that bringeth forth his fruit in his season; his leaf also shall not wither; and whatsoever he doeth shall prosper." Psalm 1:1-3

2. Make us very successful and prosperous.

"This book of the law shall not depart out of thy mouth; but thou shalt meditate therein day and night, that thou mayest observe to do according to all that is written therein: for then thou shalt make thy way prosperous, and then thou shalt have good success." Joshua 1:8

3. Cause the Holy Spirit to guide us into revelation knowledge.

"Howbeit when He, the Spirit of truth, is come, He will guide you into all truth: for He shall not speak of Himself; but whatsoever He shall hear, that shall He speak: and He will shew you things to come. He shall glorify Me: for He shall receive of Mine, and shall shew it unto you." John 16:13-14

4. Develop the Spiritual wisdom of God in us.

"But as it is written, eye hath not seen, nor ear heard, neither have entered into the heart of man, the things which God hath prepared for them that love Him. But God hath revealed them unto us by His Spirit: for the Spirit searcheth all things, yea, the deep things of God. For what man knoweth the things of a man, save the spirit of man which is in him? Even so the things of God knoweth no man, but the Spirit of God. Now we have received, not the spirit of the world, but the Spirit which is of God; that we might know the things that are freely given to us of God. Which things also we speak, not in the words which man's wisdom teacheth, but which the Holy Ghost teacheth; comparing spiritual things with spiritual." 1 Corinthians 2:9-13

5. Cause us to deal wisely in all the affairs of life.

"This Book of the Law shall not depart out of your mouth, but you shall meditate on it day and night, that you may observe and do according to all that is written in it. For then you shall make your way prosperous, and then you shall deal wisely and have good success." Joshua 1:8 (AMP)

6. Cause the Word of God to begin abiding in us, which will make our prayer lives more accurate.

"If ye abide in Me, and My Words abide in you, ye shall ask what ye will, and it shall be done unto you." John 15:7

7. Cause us to see the invisible, so we can do the impossible.

"While we look not at the things which are seen, but at the things which are not seen: for the things which are seen are temporal; but the things which are not seen are eternal." 2 Corinthians 4:18

8. Cause us to see our glorified future.

"And the Lord said unto Abram, after that Lot was separated from him, Lift up now thine eyes, and look from the place where thou art northward, and southward, and eastward, and westward: For all the land which thou seest, to thee will I give it, and to thy seed for ever." Gen 13:14-15

9. Cause us to be protected from all our enemies.

"The wicked have waited for me to destroy me: but I will consider Thy testimonies. I have seen an end of all perfection: but Thy commandment is exceeding broad. O how love I Thy law! it

is my meditation all the day. Thou through Thy commandments hast made me wiser than mine enemies: for they are ever with me. I have more understanding than all my teachers: for Thy testimonies are my meditation." Psalm 119:95-99

10. Bring us into the realm of miracles.

"Every place that the sole of your foot shall tread upon, that have I given unto you, as I said unto Moses. From the wilderness and this Lebanon even unto the great river, the river Euphrates, all the land of the Hittites, and unto the great sea toward the going down of the sun, shall be your coast. There shall not any man be able to stand before thee all the days of thy life: as I was with Moses, so I will be with thee: I will not fail thee, nor forsake thee." Joshua 1:3-5

The Law of Consistency

"Motivation gets you going; discipline keeps you growing."
John C. Maxwell

"Either make the tree good, and his fruit good; or else make the tree corrupt, and his fruit corrupt: for the tree is known by his fruit. Oh generation of vipers, how can ye, being evil, speak good things? For out of the abundance of the heart the mouth speaketh. A good man out of the good treasure of the heart brin- geth forth good things: and an evil man out of the evil treasure bringeth forth evil things. But I say unto you, that every idle word that men shall speak, they shall give account thereof in the day of judgment. For by thy words thou shalt be justified, and by thy words thou shalt be condemned." Matthew 12:33-37

The *law of consistency* says, "If you keep doing the right things in life, the right things will follow you." This is the *law of sowing and reaping*. The Scripture says, *"... of the abundance of the heart his mouth speaks," (Luke 6:45, NKJV).* If you consistently think a certain way, you will store up an abundance of that thought in your heart. Your mouth has no choice but to eventually speak out whatever is in your heart. The Amplified Bible in *Matthew 12:35* says that, *"The good man from his inner good treasure flings forth good things, and the evil man out of his inner evil storehouse flings forth evil things."* You do not even have to physically do it. Your spirit and mind will automatically fling out whatever you have consistently put in your heart.

Do you remember when the woman with the issue of blood touched the hem of Jesus' garment? The Bible says that virtue literally flung out of Him. This was able to happen because Jesus had programmed Himself with Heaven, by consistently thinking right thoughts. He created an atmosphere where the Holy Spirit could fling forth virtue from His mind and heart. Jesus did not know who touched Him, but He knew that virtue had gone out of Him. The actual Greek meaning of the word *virtue* is miracle energy. This is powerful. By consistently thinking God thoughts, Jesus produced miracle energy!

"Thou shalt also decree a thing, and it shall be established unto thee: and the light shall shine upon thy ways. When men are cast down, then thou shalt say, There is a lifting up; and He shall save the humble person." Job 22:28-29

I recently saw a man on YouTube who was not born again, but he had tapped into the law of consistency. He decided to make a dream book. In this book he listed all the nations he wanted to visit, and all the things he wanted to accomplish. Next, he chose to discipline himself for one year. In that year he consistently, and consciously refused to think any negative thoughts. He started to visualize where he wanted to be in two years. This man was not even a believer, but he set Kingdom laws in motion and they responded to him. Wow!

When I first came to Canada, I had no idea how a thermostat worked. I assumed the temperature would change immediately after I adjusted the box on the wall. This was quite frustrating because no matter how many times I moved the dial, nothing seemed to change. Then someone told me to just leave the dial alone once I had chosen a temperature. I took this advice, and do you know that a miracle took place?! I had inadvertently tapped into the *law of consistency*. I kept the dial at the desired temperature and the room began to heat up!

Once you set this powerful law in motion, do not nullify it with your thoughts, words, or actions. The man with the dream book diligently, and consistently, saw his desires coming to pass, even though in the beginning his efforts seemed insignificant. He reasoned that since the law of gravity worked for him, this law of consistency must work for him as well. A year after he began his dream book, this man's company sent him to Siberia. Siberia was not even on his list! However, he went to Siberia anyway. He made so much money there that he was able to fulfill all the things in his dream book within the next two years!

I declare, in the Name of Jesus, that the law of consistency will begin to function in your life, starting right now!

CHAPTER SIX

BELIEVE IN YOURSELF

G od does not mind you having a great value for yourself. As a matter of fact, loving yourself is not only acceptable in His eyes, but a command. In *Mark 12:30-31*, Jesus says to, *"...love the Lord thy God with all thy heart, and with all thy soul, and with all thy mind, and with all thy strength: this is the first commandment. And the second is like, namely this, Thou shalt love thy neighbour as thyself. There is none other commandment greater than these."*

We have been commanded by God to love and value ourselves. I have a very difficult time with people who think otherwise. A great American leader stated: "The best thing you can do for the poor man is not to become one yourself." In other words, do everything in your power to add value to yourself, so you can be an asset to your world and not a liability. Depression and loneliness are so prevalent today. In the last few years, we have seen an increasing number of good people committing suicide. Some of these people were even pastors and ministers. Why would a messenger of hope feel so hopeless that his thoughts would lead him to such a painful fate? I could sum it up in two words, **"No love**." Because no one cared to love them, they had no love for themselves. How sad! Let us start a love revolution by loving one person at a time, beginning with ourselves. Until we love and value ourselves, we cannot love others. Some have suggested that loving yourself is a sign of arrogance and vanity, but this is so far from the truth. Loving yourself is command.

Grow in the Confidence of Jesus

I love the Lord Jesus for many reasons, one being the confidence He exudes. No one talks and acts quite like Jesus. He is the epitome of confidence because He believes in His Father, Who works in Him. You cannot walk with Jesus and still have a poor self-image. You may start out with one, but as you begin to fellowship with Him, His confidence will be awakened in you. When this happens, you will have boldness to do anything He asks. Low self-esteem was one of the most difficult things for me to overcome as a child. I always believed that I was not good enough, or not worthy of being celebrated. However, all that changed when Jesus came! One of the first things He did was help me to see my true value. And now, one of my greatest joys in life is to help show others their own value.

My friend, when Jesus breathes His love into you and through you, His confidence and certainty will be one of the first things you notice. You will be as bold as He is, and all of Heaven will be at your disposal to help you fulfill your Kingdom assignment.

"Now when they saw the boldness of Peter and John, and perceived that they were unlearned and ignorant men, they marveled; and they took knowledge of them, that they had been with Jesus." Acts 4:13

Peter and John were under the influence of Jesus' love. That is why they had confidence to do all they set their minds to. This kind of confidence, that comes from intimacy with Jesus, is part of your inheritance! Choose to live every day with the consciousness that He has already won your victories for you. Be aware that the Word, His blood and Holy Spirit are all working on your behalf.

Change Your Internal Chatter

Internal chatter is the conversation taking place in your head. Do you criticize yourself in your thought life? If you do, please stop selling yourself short, because you do not really know who you are. God has placed greatness inside you. The reason I know this is from direct experience. He is no respecter of persons. Throughout my teenage years, I was called dumb, stupid, and hard of learning. If you had told me then what I would be doing today, I would have thought you were crazy. If God can use me, a boy from a poor village, He can use you.

Your effectiveness will increase immensely when you shut down any self-condemning and belittling conversations you have with yourself. Most of the negative conversations we have in our heads are useless. Train yourself to become aware of them and stop them, or they will become your reality. In addition to stopping negative chatter, be disciplined in speaking only positively about yourself. Also, refrain from repeating others' defeating stories about what they cannot do. I like something that Jordan Belford says in his book, *The Wolf of Wall Street*, "The only thing standing between you and your goal is the ... story you keep telling yourself as to why you cannot achieve it."

I remember when I finally told my mind to shut up. I had begun to pastor in Canada, and the negative conversation that would continually play in my head was outrageous. It would always go like this: "What are doing? You are out of your league, boy! You are not smart enough. You do not have the right qualifications, and white Canadians will not listen to a black man with an accent."

As a reinforcement to my internal conversation, when we started our church, there were no other black people in the city that I could use as inspiration. There was no T.D. Jakes, or Creflo Dollar. There was no one to motivate me. I was the black raisin in a loaf of bread, a single black face in a sea of white faces. What do you do when God calls you to such a place? Well, I quickly got over myself and just kept believing in my dreams. I told my mind to shut up, and I kept moving forward. Today, as I look back at our success in Canada, I think that only Heaven knows the tens of thousands of people who have been impacted since we came to this region. One of them is a woman who attends Living Faith:

My Yoke Was Broken

"Fourteen years ago I lived a life that was surrounded by deep depression and demonic manifestations. After crying out to God, He brought me supernaturally in contact with the ministry of Apostle Everton Weekes. My life was drastically changed after experiencing the yoke-destroying, burden-removing anointing that set me free from any trace of depression and demonic attacks. This wonderful experience caused me to move from Germany and become part of Apostle Everton's and Pastor Tracy's ministry in Canada, and attend the School of the Supernatural. Since then, my life has become full of testimonies. I have also had the privilege to travel the nations under their leadership and pray for the sick and cast out demons. Through Apostle Everton, I have also learned how to reprogram myself for success. For the very first time in my life, I was able to get rid of the limitations that have held me back all my life. For so long, I thought that I was not meant to be a business woman as I had studied 'only' social work.

Upon changing my mindset, I started to think kingdom business thoughts. All of a sudden, that little business idea I had started to grow. It appeared to be so small, but I wasn't able to shake it off anymore. In a step of faith, I went to city hall to get a business license and started my business on the side of my desk. One year later, I lost my job and wasn't able to find anything else. God provided an opportunity to receive grants for a business course. It was $14,000 in total. With this course, I was able grow my business. One Sunday service, Apostle Everton prophesied over my life that lawyers would come to seek me out, and refer their clients to me. Since then, God has continued to open tremendous doors of opportunity for me to be in contact with numerous lawyers. Clients have started to seek me out in desperation for answers to their family situations.

Today, I am at a place in my life I never thought would be possible. I came as a depressed woman to this ministry with no purpose in life. But today I have become a minister of the gospel preaching and traveling the nations. I am also a business woman who is helping many families in desperation overcome their pain, and restoring relationships through my ever growing business in family counseling and mediation." I. W.

Here is another testimony of a dear young woman whose life has been changed by our ministry.

"Growing up, I was fascinated with the healing ministry. When I first came to Living Faith Miracle Center, I watched in awe as Apostle Everton operated with such an anointing for signs and wonders. I had no idea that caliber of ministry even existed in Canada! He ministered to me as well, and God touched me powerfully. Since that day, my life has been forever changed and God has continued to transform me.

Apostle Everton has raised me up to be all that I can be, loving me through thick and thin. I remember one day I made a poor choice and instead of criticizing me, he chose to publicly defend me. He validated his love for me, getting involved in my situation and calling me higher. I cannot describe the healing this brought to my heart as I had never experienced such love before.

Apostle Everton and Pastor Tracy demonstrate the love of God, not just from the pulpit, but in their every day interactions with others. This has helped heal my heart more than words can articulate. Apostle has given me powerful prophetic words that have changed the trajectory of my life. But for me personally, the greatest impact on my life has been the opportunity and privilege to have a relationship with him and his wife. Through their lives, God has healed crevices of my heart I did not even realize were wounded, and did not want anyone to see. Through Apostle Everton and Pastor Tracy, I have been set free from the cocoon in which I kept myself imprisoned, and changed into the butterfly I was created to be. Mine is a life that is changed because this couple gave, and no words can properly articulate my gratitude." V. B.

Five Ways To Develop Belief in Yourself

1. Start believing in your dreams and God-given abilities.

If you do not believe in yourself, no one will. I like something that Robert H. Schuller once said, "If it's going to be, it's up to me." That is so true! So stop doubting your dreams and abilities. Keep believing in yourself and trusting in the potential God has placed within you. The world is full of people with lesser abilities than you, who have achieved great things. I just read a book about a man who has no arms. He drives with his legs, and combs his hair and even plays trumpet with his feet.

Now he is planning on getting his pilot's license. When I read his story something snapped inside me. There will be no more excuses for me! I will be all that God called me to be.

There are no limits–as Jesus is, so are we in this world!

2. Become God-inside minded.

"Ye are of God, little children, and have overcome them, because greater is He that is in you than he that is in the world." 1 John 4:4

The most powerful Person in the universe lives inside you! His intelligence, wisdom, strength and courage are at your disposal. My friend, you can do anything, because greater is He that is in you, than he that is in the world. Look within yourself for all the help you could ever need. Your physical body is now the temple, or dwelling place, for Jehovah. In the Old Testament, the temple had to be perfect before God. That has not changed, because God never changes. However, if the tabernacle was acceptable in the old Testament, we are much more acceptable because of Jesus' blood which cleanses us. Our tabernacle has been, and is being, perfected by Christ.

"For by a single offering He has forever completely cleansed and perfected those who are consecrated and made holy." Hebrews 10:14 (AMP)

You have become the perfect dwelling place for God because of your union with Christ. Stop and think about that for a moment! If God, the most righteous Judge, believes in you so much that He chose to live in you, why is it so difficult for you to believe in yourself? Make it your quest to discover the Master Who dwells within you. He is the one who can change anything in a moment. Never believe satan, or allow him to feed you with negative thoughts concerning your value in God's Kingdom.

3. Speak your beliefs and dreams regularly.

One of the fastest ways to stop self-limiting beliefs is to begin speaking to your potential. A trademark of successful people is, they always speak to where they are going. They do this because they believe in themselves. I encourage you to think big and start declaring where you want to go in life. The best future you can have is the one you help create. Open your mouth wide, let the Lord fill your mouth with wisdom, and begin to shape the world around you. Jesus said, *"For verily I say unto you, That whosoever shall say unto this mountain, Be thou removed, and be thou cast into the sea; and shall not doubt in his heart, but shall believe that those things which he saith shall come to pass; he shall have whatsoever he saith,"* *(Mark 11:23)*.

Be warned, some people may become angry with you when you start declaring your dreams, but do not worry about that. Just be like Joseph and keep on talking. Your critics are just an indication that you are on the right track. Have you ever noticed that people who are not doing anything rarely get criticized? So keep talking and keep believing.

4. Trust in the Lord to build your confidence.

When you are trusting God, it is impossible to not believe in the life He has placed in you. The life of God is your ticket to the land of plenty. In every situation where you place your trust in God, you are building your confidence in Him. You are also solidifying your dreams and belief systems. Child of God, the more you trust the Lord, the more you believe in yourself.

"Those who trust in the Lord are as Mount Zion, which cannot be moved but abides forever. As the mountains surround Jerusalem, So the Lord surrounds His people from this time forth and forever." Psalm 125:1-2 (NASB)

"The fear of man bringeth a snare, but whoso putteth his trust in the Lord shall be safe." Proverbs 29:25

5. Look for opportunities to be a big giver.

What you make happen for others, God will make happen for you. Practice putting smiles on people's faces! Make it your habit to keep money in your pocket and look for opportunities to be a Boaz to someone. There are things I am trusting God for, so I need as much help as possible. As long as I live, I will be a big Kingdom giver. I know that, *"...whatsoever good thing any man doeth, the same shall he receive of the Lord, whether he be bond or free," (Ephesians 6:8).* Heaven responds to you, as you respond to the Heaven in you.

As we close this chapter, allow me to leave you with one last thought:

To the degree you value and believe in yourself, will be the degree that people value and believe in you.

CHAPTER SEVEN

YOU WERE BORN TO BE GREAT

"I call Heaven and Earth to record this day against you, that I have set before you life and death, blessing and cursing: therefore choose life, that both thou and thy seed may live." Deuteronomy 30:19

God has placed greatness inside of you. Therefore the choice for you to be great is not yours, but His. Every challenge you face is just another opportunity for that greatness to manifest.

"May the Lord, the God of your fathers, make you a thousand times as many as you are and bless you as He has promised you!" Deuteronomy 1:11 (AMP)

"And they blessed Rebekah, and said unto her, Thou art our sister, be thou the mother of thousands of millions, and let thy seed possess the gate of those which hate them." Genesis 24:60

"Then the Lord took Abram outside and said to him, Look up into the sky and count the stars if you can. That's how many descendants you will have!" Genesis 15:5 (NLT)

Now, I know these Scriptures are talking about the nation of Israel. However, by faith we can make them ours, because we are indeed the true sons and daughters of Abraham. More importantly, we are the sons and daughters of the most high God, the Creator of Heaven and Earth. Based on the Scriptures above, I would like to introduce you to four powerful principles about God that will help to destroy the spirit of failure in your life.

Four Power Principles

1. **God has a large vision for His people. He does not want us to think small.**

2. **Thinking small limits God, and therefore limits us.**

3. **God wants us to make room for Him in our imaginations.**

4. **God wants us to be greater than those who have gone before us.**

Your mindset is the secret to your success. Throughout history, great men and women with lesser ability than yours have experienced failure. However, because they refused to see themselves as failures, they overcame obstacles that seemed to be insurmountable at the time. The Bible says that God wants us to be a thousand times greater than them. The question is, "Who are these people?" They are people who inspire us, and motivate us to be great. They challenge us to become the best possible version of ourselves.

Biblical Fathers Who Challenge Us To Be Great

"The LORD God of your fathers make you a thousand times so many more as ye are, and bless you, as he hath promised you!" (Deuteronomy 1:11).

89

The Word also tells us to, *"...Be not slothful, but followers of them who through faith and patience inherit the promises,"* *(Hebrews 6:12)*.

1. Abraham, the Father of Faith

Abraham's life of faith caused him to become a friend of God.

"And being not weak in faith, he considered not his own body now dead, when he was about an hundred years old, neither yet the deadness of Sarah's womb: He staggered not at the promise of God through unbelief; but was strong in faith, giving glory to God; And being fully persuaded that, what He had promised, He was able also to perform." (Romans 4:19-21).

"And the scripture was fulfilled which saith, Abraham believed God, and it was imputed unto him for righteousness: and he was called the friend of God." (James 2:23).

2. David, the beloved King of Israel

No one in the Israelite army thought that faith in God could kill Goliath. David eliminated him though, with just a slingshot, five smooth stones, and faith. David also won every Kingdom battle he every fought, because he trusted in his God. Now this is powerful, and it is our inheritance. Think about this – every battle King David ever fought, he won! And God wants us to be one thousand times greater. Wow!

"Then David said to the Philistine, You come to me with a sword, with a spear, and with a javelin. But I come to you in the name of the Lord of hosts, the God of the armies of Israel, whom you have defied." 1 Samuel 17:45 (NKJV)

3. Elijah, the Prophet

Who thought Elijah's mighty prayers could cause the heavens to give rain? Elijah was a man with a nature like ours. However, he prayed earnestly that it would not rain, and it did not rain on the earth for three and a half years. After he had an opportunity to prove to the people who God is, he prayed again, and the rain came pouring down.

"Elias was a man subject to like passions as we are, and he prayed earnestly that it might not rain: and it rained not on the earth by the space of three years and six months. And he prayed again, and the heaven gave rain, and the earth brought forth her fruit." James 5:17-18

4. Solomon, King of Israel

God gave Solomon wisdom when he asked for it, and the Bible says that he was the wisest man who ever lived. He wrote close to three thousand proverbs, and composed over one thousand songs.

"When the queen of Sheba saw all the wisdom of Solomon and the palace he had built, the food on his table, the seating of his officials, the attending servants in their robes, his cupbearers, and the burnt offerings he made at the temple of the Lord, she was overwhelmed. She said to the king, The report I heard in my own country about your achievements and your wisdom is true. But I did not believe these things until I came and saw with my own eyes. Indeed, not even half was told me; in wisdom and wealth you have far exceeded the report I heard. How happy your people must be! How happy your officials, who continually stand before you and hear your wisdom!" 1 Kings 10:4-8 (NIV)

5. Moses, deliverer of the children of Israel

By faith, Moses delivered five million people from slavery without a sword!

"He brought them forth also with silver and gold: and there was not one feeble person among their tribes. Egypt was glad when they departed: for the fear of them fell upon them. He spread a cloud for a covering; and fire to give light in the night. The people asked, and He brought quails, and satisfied them with the bread of Heaven. He opened the rock, and the waters gushed out; they ran in the dry places like a river. For He remembered His holy promise, and Abraham His servant. And He brought forth His people with joy, and His chosen with gladness: and gave them the lands of the heathen: and they inherited the labor of the people." Psalm 105:37-44

Modern Day Leaders Who Challenge Us To Be Great

1. Called a slow learner, mentally challenged, and even written off as illiterate and you will have an Albert Einstein.

2. A scientist who failed over ten thousand times in his experiments with a light bulb and you will have a Thomas Edison.

3. Called a gorilla, buffoon, and even an embarrassment to the republic, and you will have an Abraham Lincoln, one of America's greatest presidents.

4. Went broke seven times, had one nervous breakdown, and lost his job because he was not creative enough, and you will have a Walt Disney.

5. Born black in a nation filled with racial discrimination, and told that she should sit at the back of the bus and you will have a Rosa Parks.

6. Told he would never amount to anything in life when in high school, and gradually went deaf as a young man in his twenties, and you will have a Ludwig van Beethoven, the genius composer.

When I look at that list of leaders I realize how dark society would have been without their contributions to life. This fills my heart with such hope, because God says He wants us to be a thousand times greater than them. Child of God, it is time for you to shine! It is time for you to break forth into your highest potential. Failure and limitation are not for you, because you are born of God.

Ways to Become Great!

1. Get tired of yourself.

Become tired of the way you are living, and tired of being broke. Get tired of making plans for something better, and then lacking the drive to see it come to pass. Get tired of being sick, and tired of just surviving.

I became so tired of being poor. I remember the embarrassment I felt one day when my wife went to the store, only to find out at the checkout that the bank card was rejected because of insufficient funds. I vowed that would never happen again! I remember also when our electricity and telephone were disconnected because we did not have any money to meet our obligations. I did not understand how on the one hand I could pray and open blind eyes, or move mountains in the lives of people, but on the other hand lack the wisdom to make money. Something was wrong with this picture!

My friend, the principles I am sharing with you in this book are not new. But they only work for those who practice them. What you need to do is locate where you are at. Then you must believe that God has something better for you. His vision for you is to be a thousand times greater than those who have gone before you. Child of God, you have to hate your present pain in order for things to change. My pastor used to say that until you hate your Egypt, you will not be qualified for your promised land. In other words, you must get tired of your circumstances for your life to change. Change will only come when you change. So stop looking for change, and be the change that you need.

First of all, you must develop a strategy. All changes take place first in the mind. Then, picture your desires being fulfilled. Just like grass grows little by little, changes will come if you stick with your desired mental pictures. For example, if you desire to lose weight, see yourself as slim and fit. Then, start to eat smaller portions, and go for a walk or a bike ride. Do not hurt yourself by going to the extreme. Just keep moving! By taking little steps, you can achieve your goals. God will help you win in this area!

2. Find the right company.

Finding the right company is one of the keys that that will unlock your greatness. It is so important for you to surround yourself with people whom you aspire to be like. Some people will only celebrate you when everything seems to be going good, but in times of crisis, their support for you dwindles. Those are not the type of people you need in your life. I am so glad that Daniel and his friends had a different spirit:

"Then Daniel went to his house, and made the thing known to Hananiah, Mishael, and Azariah, his companions: That they would desire mercies of the God of Heaven concerning this secret; that Daniel and his fellows should not perish with the rest of the wise men of Babylon Then was the secret revealed unto Daniel in a night vision. Then Daniel blessed the God of Heaven." Daniel 2:17-19

"Do not be misled: Bad company corrupts good character." 1 Corinthians 15:33 (NIV)

"He that walketh with wise men shall be wise: but a companion of fools shall be destroyed." Proverbs 13:20

A major factor to our success in life hinges on our ability to terminate wrong relationships, and to spend time associating with quality people who will take us to the next level. It is vital that we understand this principle. Secrets are revealed in the presence of the right company. Until you find the right people, your destiny can be held hostage. My friend, not everyone should be close to you. Choose the right inner circle if you desire to be one thousand times greater.

The Bible is full of companies: David, Paul, Job, and even Jesus all had theirs. Your company determines both your longevity and your staying power in the course of destiny. You can only go as far as the people you associate with. They make or break you.

God, in His wisdom, knows more about us than we know about ourselves. The choice, however, remains with us to stay well-connected to our God-given company. God knows what we will face; He knows our struggles! He also knows who can best encourage us, which is why we need to drink from the wells where He has planted us.

3. Have clear, written goals.

A goal that is not in writing is just a wish. A dream without goals will only lead to frustration. I have met so many people over the years who are full of all kinds of dreams. I often ask them what their goals or plans are for bringing about their dreams. In response, people frequently look at me with disdain as if to say, "What planet are you from, brother?" They seem to think that it is God's job to manifest their dreams.

Having that kind of attitude is like saying your grass needs cutting, but that is okay, because God will cut it for you. Now I believe in miracles, so I would never say God will not cut you grass. However, if He does, please give Him my address because mine needs cutting too. Now, I know I am being funny, but my point here is to show you that God does not work that way. When He gives you a dream, He expects you to get involved in manifesting that dream. There will be elements of your dream that only God can bring to pass. Mostly though, you just have to get involved and do your part. Once you begin to do your part, God will work behind the scenes to bring about His part.

Having a Dream is not Enough.

After deciding on your dreams, you need to develop a strategy to realize those dreams. Jim Carrey is a famous Canadian actor and comedian. When he was broke, Mr. Carrey wrote himself a cheque for $10 million and put it in his wallet. Then he told his friends that one day he would cash the cheque. That was his dream. Then, he started doing odd jobs acting here and there. What was he doing? Trying to cash that cheque. Eventually, in 1994, Jim Carrey had one of the most successful years in Hollywood history. He hit it big time that year when he was given the star role in three of the funniest movies of all time: *Ace Ventura: Pet Detective, The Mask*, and *Dumb and Dumber.*

According to Wikipedia, each film was a bigger hit than the last. Altogether they pulled in more than $700 million worldwide. So tell me, do you think Jim Carrey cashed that cheque? You better believe it! Today (according to celebritynetworth.com), his net worth is $150 million.

What is your dream? Is it to be a teacher, minister, fireman, or lawyer? What is on your heart? When you find your dream, please do not make the mistake of sitting on the sidelines, waiting for something magical to happen. You have to develop a strategy that will put legs on your dreams.

Do you know what separates dreamers from doers? Clearly written goals. Yes, you heard me. You need to write them down. I am very passionate about goals. My goals are my life. My goals are my future on paper. That is why I dedicate one day a week just to work on my goals. The Lord showed me something beautiful about goal writing that changed my life. He told me if I will write out my goals, His angel will run with them. In the book of *Habakkuk 2:2-3*, we are told, *"And the Lord answered me, and said, Write the vision, and make it plain upon tables, that he may run that readeth it. For the vision is yet for an appointed time, but at the end it shall speak, and not lie: though it tarry, wait for it; because it will surely come, it will not tarry."*

Write the Vision down. Make it plain. That they that read it may run with it.

Then God told me to never limit the fulfillment of my dreams to the actions of people. He has committed His angel to run with my clearly written goals. This revelation came to me years ago. Since that time, I have seen so many miracles in my life. One year, we saw over $20,000 in debts paid off and canceled. Debt that had been around for years was miraculously paid off! Why did this happen? Because I made the vision plain, and God's angel kept running to bring it into manifestation.

My thirteen year old son, Joshua, also set this principle in motion. Take a look at his results. Joshua was trusting the Lord for a new laptop. He did two things. First, he planted a seed. Then, for forty-two days straight, he faithfully wrote his prayers out, thanking the Lord for his new laptop. On his birthday last year, he received his desired harvest. The Holy Spirit is no respecter of persons. If He answers the prayers of a thirteen year old, He will do the same for you.

4. Become glory conscious.

Greatness can also come into your life because of your connection to the God of glory. In these last days, God is removing shame, and garnishing His people with His glory. In the book of Joel we are told, *"And ye shall eat in plenty, and be satisfied, and praise the name of the Lord your God, that hath dealt wondrously with you: and My people shall never be ashamed. And ye shall know that I am in the midst of Israel, and that I am the Lord your God, and none else: and My people shall never be ashamed," (Joel 2:26-27).* This is so beautiful. Here you can see how God is using His glory to distinguish His people from the world.

Throughout the Old Testament, God separated His people for distinction using blood, gold and favor. For example, in Genesis, we see how Jacob was cheated out of his wages for fourteen years. He was living in extreme poverty. However, the God of glory came on the scene and everything changed. *"And the man increased exceedingly, and had much cattle, and maidservants, and menservants, and camels, and asses," (Genesis 30:43).*

God is ready to do the same thing for you and your family. When God rests His glory on you, it will launch you into uncommon progress. Dead dreams will bud again. Red Seas will be crossed, and even dead things will come back to life. Over the last several years, I can testify to such distinctions. I have seen the Lord do things in our lives and ministry that have brought tears of joy to my eyes. Things that would normally take years, took days. When the glory came upon Joseph, he went from the prison to the palace in one day. Child of God, it is time for you to become glory conscious. Start looking for glory friends, and seek out glory meetings. Be part of a glory church.

The book you are holding was birthed out of a glory service in Switzerland that lasted eight hours. There was a woman in that meeting who had experienced twelve miscarriages. God miraculously touched her, and a few months later, she had a bouncing baby boy. Also, legs that were short grew out, and the deaf heard for the first time. Many, many healings and miracles took place. One man, who had been unemployed for two years, now has his own business. You see my friends, when the glory manifests, there is always an acceleration. The glory is an accelerator!

God is accelerating everything in these last days. So, get ready to experience His greatness as you press into His glory.

5. Refuse to be afraid.

"Do what you fear, and fear will disappear."
David Joseph Schwartz

Many people become paralyzed because of fear. In fact, fear has stopped millions of people from doing what they know they should do. Webster defines fear as believing and expecting the worst to happen. It can be the anticipation of evil, or fear that something bad will happen. The Bible calls fear a spirit. So fear is more than something psychological; fear is a demonic spirit. This evil spirit is an enemy of God, and a destroyer of destinies.

As you can see, the reason people expect the worst out of life is because their mind is under attack by an evil spirit. Announce aloud with me three times: **"I refuse to be afraid."** If fear is not dealt with, it can create a nervous breakdown, and sickness in the body. Job said, *"For the thing which I greatly feared is come upon me, and that which I was afraid of is come unto me,"* *(Job 3:25)*. This is powerful. Job's imaginations became his reality. Child of God, if a negative imagination can become a living reality, the opposite is also true. Stop fear! Fear is not in your nature. You are called to manifest the glory of God.

Five Practical Ways to Overcome Fear

1. Isolate your fear and pin it down.

Determine exactly what you are afraid of. Then take bold action against that fear. Do not hesitate, for hesitation only enlarges the fear. Face fear, because it is only in your imagination.

2. Be a front seater. Every time you sit at the back, you feed your fear. Sitting up front builds confidence.

3. Practice making eye contact. How a person uses their eyes tell a lot about them. Failure to make eye contact is one of two things: either you feel weak beside the other person, or you feel inferior to him. Child of God, you are a king. You have nothing to be afraid of. Greater is He that is in you, than he that is in the world.

4. Smile big and you will feel big. Smile until your teeth show. You will be amazed at the results a simple smile can bring.

5. Practice speaking clearly, and with confidence. Confidence is the backbone of a champion, so never be afraid.

Ways Fear can Be Destroyed

Have a consistent prayer life.
"I sought the Lord, and He heard me, and delivered me from all my fears." Psalm 34:4

Actively put your trust and confidence in God.
"In God have I put my trust: I will not be afraid what man can do unto me." Psalm 56:11

Make a quality decision that you will boldly confront and steadfastly resist all fears. *"Submit yourselves therefore to God. Resist the devil, and he will flee from you." James 4:7*

Praise God continually. *"I will bless the Lord at all times: His praise shall continually be in my mouth." Psalm 34:1*

Actively walk in the love of God. God's divine love drives out all fear. *"There is no fear in love; but perfect love casteth out fear: because fear hath torment. He that feareth is not made perfect in love." 1 John 4:18*

Use the mighty weapons God has given you. *"For though we walk in the flesh, we do not war after the flesh. For the weapons of our warfare are not carnal, but mighty through God to the pulling down of strong holds; Casting down imaginations, and every high thing that exalteth itself against the knowledge of God, and bringing into captivity every thought to the obedience of Christ." 2 Corinthians 10:3-5*

CHAPTER EIGHT

THE POWER OF FOCUS

F ocus can be described as concentration at its best. The one who masters focus can enhance his destiny. A person with the ability to concentrate can accomplish anything. The Bible tells us that, *"The light of the body is the eye: if therefore thine eye be single, thy whole body shall be full of light,"* *(Matthew 6:22).*

Focus is powerful. Singleness of vision releases tremendous power. If you are a person with a million things on the go and no particular passion for any one of them, I can predict your progress and success in five minutes. To be scattered is to dilute your power. In the past, I have made the mistake of doing too much, too soon, and it cost me dearly. Please understand this guy called Everton Weekes – I am not a normal person. I am a visionary, a go-getter, someone who likes to be in control, and who believes the world is often too slow. I become disturbed at the thought of sitting around for too long doing nothing. I despise laziness, and have little mercy for mediocrity when I see it. Thankfully, God has given me a good wife who keeps me balanced.

When you locate that one thing God has called you to do, go ahead and do it with all your heart. You can be sure your desired results will come. Remember, your life goes in the direction of your focus. Where focus goes, energy flows – whether that energy is negative or positive. I once heard a great man of God say that the only way satan can defeat you is by succeeding in breaking your focus. How true!

Webster defines *focus* as, directing your attention or effort at something specific. If your internal focus is sharp and precise, the implementation of your vision will surely move forward. Focus is to vision, what a compass is to a ship. A ship without a compass will travel aimlessly and never arrive at any precise destination. Proper focus will give direction and momentum to your dream.

Our opening Scripture says that if your eye is single, your whole body will be full of light. A single eye speaks of focus, and focus attracts blessings. These may come in the form of opportunities and open doors. I have been in the ministry now for over fifteen years and this principle of focus attracting opportunities has born much fruit in my life. We have traveled to many nations, and counseled world leaders. We have seen over fifty thousand people attend our conferences and miracle crusades. We have also held panel discussions with top medical doctors concerning how the sick can be healed. Hundreds of thousands have been healed, saved and brought into a life of victory in Christ. I give all the glory to God for this, because I can never forget where God brought me from. I was a little boy with a stammering tongue, who was not supposed to amount to anything good in life. My life is proof that with God anything is possible, and what He has done for me, He can do for you!

Give Yourself a Chance To See what God can Do

Some people never give God a chance to establish their goings. They quit on their dreams because the process is too slow. We are living in a get rich quick generation: "Give it to me now – I have to go!" This mentality has become the downfall of many. Do not let this be your story! Every good and successful enterprise will take time to bear fruit.

A good friend of mine recently shared something with me that illustrates this. One of his leaders was caught in a very immoral act. He told me he met with the man and agreed to help restore him. My friend devised a plan of restoration, in which he would help this man be restored in seven months. However, in that period of time he would not be allowed to minister publicly. Sadly, the man refused to participate in the restoration plan because he was too proud to endure a seven month process. Four years have now gone by since this happened, and the man has still not been restored. He has lost credibility in the city and now his life is in a worse state than when he started. How sad!

My friend, in the little experience that my life has given me, I have learned one thing. Those who fight against the process for success take longer to fulfill their dreams, if they still have a dream. But happy are those who stay the course, having the law of focus working for them. I remember in the early days when my wife and I had to pass this test. Our pastor asked us to start a Bible study in a certain area of town, and for months, often only two or three people would show up. I still remember this very well because one of the men would come drunk, and the other had mild schizophrenia. This was my welcome to ministry. There were many months when we would drive forty-five minutes to meetings – just to minister to a handful of people. I remember sitting in a home in Boston, teaching Bible study to the few faithful who came, only to be interrupted by the sound of gun shots. This was our welcome to Massachusetts. Today, as I look back on our early beginnings, I thank God for His wisdom in teaching me this great law of focus.

When focus is combined with a Godly desire, divine energy is released. I want to share with you the story of a man of God in the Bible who was broke and defeated for almost fifteen years. Jacob worked faithfully without receiving adequate wages. One day, in the middle of his pain, he decided to do something about his situation. This story always troubles me because Jacob was a man who loved God. Yet, with all that love, God did not even try and help him one time.

This is shocking! We can learn from this story that until you change your focus, not even God can help you. Let us read about Jacob in *Genesis 30:26-30:*

"Give me my wives and my children, for whom I have served thee, and let me go: for thou knowest my service which I have done thee. And Laban said unto him, I pray thee, if I have found favor in thine eyes, tarry: for I have learned by experience that the Lord hath blessed me for thy sake. And he said, Appoint me thy wages, and I will give it. And he said unto him, Thou knowest how I have served thee, and how thy cattle were with me. For it was little which thou had before I came, and it is now increased unto a multitude; and the Lord hath blessed thee since my coming: and now when shall I provide for mine own house also?"

I like this very much. Jacob says, "I have worked for you, but there is no proof of my personal success." Jacob was not a lazy man, but his focus was in the wrong place. He was making his boss rich, at his expense. This went on for almost fifteen years. Finally, he became tired of living below his covenant right, and he decided to change his focus. The moment he did this, God brought him into unlimited wealth.

"Thus the man became exceedingly prosperous, and had large flocks, female and male servants, and camels and donkeys."
Genesis 30:43 (NKJV)

Until you focus on your gift, you will live life like a dog, always depending on your master for food. I know this is a strong statement, but it's the truth! Stop drifting, because the blessing only comes when you are focused. There are many drifters in the world. Today, it is time for you to stand out by doing something that will shake you out of your comfort zone. God is calling you to stay focused on your gift and keep doing the thing He has assigned you to do.

I have seen a lot of craziness! For example, in the early days of my ministry, I was called to help a certain church. The pastors there were conference junkies. Every few months they would attend another conference, and when they returned, they would change the direction of their church. One day, they invited us to come do a conference on the supernatural. But what they learned from us was short-lived, for they soon went on to something they considered newer and better. How sad! They could never focus on the one thing God told them to do, and I don't think that church ever did get established.

You see, the things of God require time to take root. You have to be patient enough to let it happen. The Bible says the Kingdom of God is like a seed. We can also say it this way: The ways of God are like seeds. They must be planted before the desired harvest can come. What would you think of a farmer who dug up his planted seed before it could grow and mature, and then became angry with God because he did not see any harvest?

Many have destroyed their ministry and business because they have violated this law of focus. Pastor Tracy and I have made up our minds to stay true to the mandate God gave us *to Raise up a generation of believers who will walk daily in the power of God*. We are called to plant breakthrough churches, have schools of the supernatural and *Born to Win* conferences, and hold mass crusades where millions will be saved and discipled. This is what we do, because it is our mandate!

The great man of God, T. L Osborn, was still doing mass crusades a month before he went to Heaven. He ministered in this way for seventy years, faithfully preaching the gospel and healing the sick. He stuck with his assignment through to the very end of his time on earth.

Evangelist Billy Graham has remained focused on the message of salvation God gave him from the very beginning of his ministry. When the charismatic and healing wave came, he just continued preaching salvation. Around the time Oral Roberts built his university, someone gave Billy Graham a large parcel of land so that he could build a university as well. He had money, teachers, and crowds. But when he talked to God about it, the Lord said, "This is not part of your assignment," so Billy Graham dropped the idea. What a joy it is today, to see him listed among the top six people who have changed the twentieth century! So many people are enjoying Heaven now because he stayed the course. What a man! May God help us all to do the same and remain faithful to, and focused on, our callings.

CHAPTER NINE

THE ME I SEE, IS THE ME I WILL BE

"A strong, positive self-image is the best possible preparation
for success."
Dr. Joyce Brothers

*"And there we saw the giants, the sons of Anak, which come
of the giants: and we were in our own sight as grasshoppers,
and so we were in their sight." Numbers 13:33*

*"And He brought forth His people with joy, and His chosen
with gladness: And gave them the lands of the heathen:
and they inherited the labour of the people; that they might
observe His statutes, and keep His laws. Praise ye the Lord."
Psalm 105:43-45*

The way you see yourself in your imagination has a tremendous impact on every area of your life. This reflection of your own feeling of worth is called your self-image. It is the degree to which you like and value yourself in your skin. When the children of Israel were first delivered out of slavery, they had a problem seeing themselves as successful. God saw them as owners of lands, cities, houses and vineyards. They saw themselves as slaves, and they died without entering their promised land. The next generation inherited the promise. If you, like the Israelites, cannot see and agree with what God says about you, you will never walk in His plans for you. Now is definitely the time to wake up and believe the Gospel!

Do not Die a Slave When You Were Born To Be a King

"And it shall be, when the Lord thy God shall have brought thee into the land which He sware unto thy fathers, to Abraham, to Isaac, and to Jacob, to give thee great and goodly cities, which thou buildedst not, and houses full of all good things, which thou filledst not, and wells digged, which thou diggedst not, vineyards and olive trees, which thou plantedst not; when thou shalt have eaten and be full; then beware lest thou forget the Lord, which brought thee forth out of the land of Egypt, from the house of bondage." Deuteronomy 6:10-12

In this chapter we are going to deal with some issues that tend to be deeply rooted. Listen, although God delivered the children of Israel from the land of bondage, He could not deliver them from the bondage of their minds. Maybe you have never seen it this way before. What God thinks and says about you is very important, but what you think and say about yourself determines your success in life. My friend, do not be deceived by what religion and small-minded people may have taught you. A healthy self-image is vital to your success. The mental picture you hold of yourself not only determines how far you will go in life, but also how happy you will be along the way. This is why the little devil is on a mission to keep you small in your imagination. The devil plans negative circumstances for you, designed to weaken your mind. The choices you make and the type of people in your life are the fruit of self-image, for better or worse, and the little devil knows this very well. That is why it is so important to watch and guard your mind! Feed your soul with right thoughts and words.

God Wants You To Be the Head, not the Tail

"And the Lord will make you the head and not the tail; you shall be above only, and not be beneath, if you heed the commandments of the Lord your God, which I command you today, and are careful to observe them." Deuteronomy 28:13 (NKJV)

"And it shall be, when the Lord thy God shall have brought thee into the land which He sware unto thy fathers, to Abraham, to Isaac, and to Jacob, to give thee great and goodly cities, which thou buildedst not, and houses full of all good things, which thou filledst not, and wells digged, which thou diggedst not, vineyards and olive trees, which thou plantedst not; when thou shalt have eaten and be full; then beware lest thou forget the Lord, which brought thee forth out of the land of Egypt, from the house of bondage." Deuteronomy 6:10-12

Does this Scripture sound too good to apply to you? Please do not fight this, just receive it! Just act like God knows what He is talking about! When was the last time you did something good for yourself?

Child of God, I declare that greatness is beginning to rain on you! You are called to be the head and not the tail.

Let this be your mental portrait for the rest of your life. Let this image of favor and success form your attitude toward yourself and those around you. You are called to believe and agree with God's favorable assessment of you – and your mission in life is to bring many people to the top with you. I believe that is the reason you were chosen to hear this good news. Millions have never heard what you are hearing right now. Oh, please receive and live by these gracious words, because they are God's way of saying to you:

**"I love you!
I created My best when I created you!
I paid a price for you, and you are worth it all!
I have destined My best for you!" (Dr. T .L. Osborn)**

Nothing Is Too Good for You if You Can Just See Your Worth

"From now on, brothers and sisters, if anything is excellent and if anything is admirable, focus your thoughts on these things: all that is true, all that is holy, all that is just, all that is pure, all that is lovely, and all that is worthy of praise. Practice these things: whatever you learned, received, heard, or saw in us. The God of peace will be with you." Philippians 4:8-9 (CEB)

How do you see? You see with your mind; your thoughts are the seeds of mental pictures, images or visions. Thoughts contain worlds, possibilities, ideas, concepts, feelings, emotions and imaginations. When your mind is impregnated with a thought, good or bad, everything embedded in that thought is released into your system.

The Power of Thoughts

Many negative events and influences can occur in life, and these can stain your mind with a sense of limitation or failure. Our minds need to be washed clean from every restriction. The Bible tells us to, *"... be renewed in the spirit of your mind," (Ephesians 4:23)*. If you can see something good within yourself, know that you can have or achieve that good thing.

Thoughts are extremely powerful! We just spoke of what your thoughts contain. To reprogram your life for success you must first change your thoughts. The day I grasped this truth was the day I discovered that no one can stop me from becoming a success. The only person who can stop you is the person in the mirror; the devil is not your problem. Your thoughts can either bring you into liberty, or hold you in mental bondage.

When I came to Canada years ago, I had a very strong accent – much stronger than it is today. Everywhere I went, people would tell me I had an accent – as if I was oblivious to that fact! Later, I discovered the reason some of those people spoke to me that way. They were really trying to limit me. They were insinuating that my accent indicated I lacked intelligence, and so I would not be able to do certain things. How sad! I became very self-conscious of my voice, and then I became withdrawn, even to the point of being afraid to speak. The more I spoke, the more I hated myself. I found myself starting to take on these limitations of my critics, and fulfilling their prophecies about me. I actually began to believe that because I had an accent there were certain things I could not achieve. Interestingly, when I began to reprogram myself with thoughts of success, I started to see my accent as an asset. Now, I see my accent as heavenly, and when you go to Heaven you will sound just like me! I am just informing you now, so you will not have a culture shock!

Your thoughts can make or break you. Everything you see on Earth was once a thought. In fact, this book you are reading right now was once only a thought. Never allow the thoughts of other people to prevent you from pursuing your dreams. Many times people will try to impose their convictions on you. They will try to make their limitations become your standard. When another man's limitations become your standard, you have a problem. For example, if you allow the doctors' limiting prognoses to become your thoughts, your stronghold, or your mindset, you have just trapped yourself in a world of sickness and problems.

Take the Limits Off God and Yourself

"Yea, they turned back and tempted God, and limited the Holy One of Israel. They remembered not His hand, nor the day when He delivered them from the enemy. How He had wrought His signs in Egypt, and His wonders in the field of Zoan." Psalm 78:41-43

Every time you either limit yourself, or allow others to limit you, your flow of creativity is restrained. When creativity stops flowing, God's nature in you is hindered from manifesting. God is calling you into the realm of progress. You must keep pressing forward. Every time you sense limitation, you have to rise up against it, because restriction and disadvantage do not come from God.

Limitation presents itself in many different ways, which you need to recognize. Parents, teachers or doctors may try to limit you, but mostly, limitation comes through your own thoughts. Periodically we all experience some measure of negativity, but how we handle negative thoughts or circumstances determines the kind of lives we will live. The doctor may have just given you a bad report, but do not receive it!

God's Word is your report. Jesus is not a liar! He told the truth when He said that with His stripes you are healed. Do you have fear about your future? I have good news for you! God's Word says, *"Fear not, little flock, it is your Father's good pleasure to give you the Kingdom," (Luke 12:32)*. The question we all have to ask ourselves is, "Whose report will I believe?"

Your problem is not the doctor, the teachers, Jesus, or the devil. The problem is your thoughts. Your thoughts shape your world. This applies equally to both men and women. Some people will say that women are disqualified from earning certain amounts of money. Ladies, why not just surprise them by manifesting such amazing wealth, they have nothing more to say! Everything in life originates in your thoughts. I am here to tell you that no one can stop you. The devil is not strong enough to stop you, so he is out of the equation. God is on your side. You are the only person who can stop you, by clinging to your negative thoughts. But I have good news! Wrong thoughts can be dissolved.

What Are Thoughts?

Thoughts are pictures in your mind that have constructive or destructive possibilities. They have emotions. They are more than imagination; they are deliberate. You think them up, construct them, and shape them. With your thoughts, you create the world you are presently living in, so if you do not like what you see, you can change it now.

Years ago, I read a book called *As a Man Thinketh*, by James Allen. This writing is a must read for any real student of success. Mr. Allen states, "Your subconscious cannot distinguish between imagination, dreams or reality." Wow! He teaches that if, on a regular basis, you provide your mind with a clear picture of your goal, your subconscious will create circumstances that will bring about the manifestation of that goal. My friend, your mind is gift from God. You are to use it to fulfill your glorious destiny, which in turn will bring Him pleasure and honor.

Remember what we have discussed so far; everything created began as a thought, and thoughts can be either creative or destructive. I once heard of a rare case where a man died from hypothermia in the middle of summer. Hypothermia is a condition where the body's internal mechanisms cannot replenish heat being lost, and core temperature falls below what is necessary to sustain life. This dear man died, shivering and mentally confused.

The mystery for those investigating his death was, how could such a thing happen during the warmest time of year? So what did cause this man to get hypothermia in the middle of summer – what caused his body temperature to fall so low that he lost the ability to warm himself in the middle of summer? His thoughts! The fearful thoughts he dwelt upon and fed to his subconscious created the unhealthy circumstance which led to his death.

The Nature of Thoughts

Thoughts carry with them emotions associated with their source. Whatever we meditate on will release either poison into our bodies, or health. Everything depends on the source of our thoughts.

Thoughts have creative abilities. This is why we need to intentionally take the thoughts associated with God's Words and design the world we want to live in. We do this with our thoughts.

Thoughts have personality and emotions. The Holy Spirit told me years ago to never be a victim of atmospheres! He said, "Whenever you enter a house, car, plane, or any other place, always take control over the present atmosphere." So whenever I go to someone's house, I say, "Peace in this house," and as I do that, I project my thoughts into the room.

Thoughts are a spiritual force. They can move mountains out of the way, or dissolve them into nothing. Because spiritual laws are superior to the physical, when the spiritual comes into this physical world, it brings change.

Thoughts Have Intelligence

Thoughts are powerful. A Japanese scientist conducted an interesting experiment. He set out two bowls of rice; bowl A and bowl B. Then he spoke words over rice-bowl A, "You are ugly, you are stupid, and you are foolish!" Over rice-bowl B he said, "You are beautiful, you are sweet!" After two weeks of repeating this exercise daily, he made an amazing discovery. The bowl of rice he spoke negative words over became dark and ugly with mold. The other bowl he spoke sweet words over was beautiful.

The scientist then decided to conduct the same type of experiment using only thoughts, rather than words. He set out two glasses of water, and with his thoughts he would think and focus. Remember, thoughts have constructive possibilities. He would think these thoughts: "Glass of water A, you are beautiful, and B, you are ugly." After two weeks of just projecting his thoughts towards the glasses of water, he obtained the same results as with his rice-bowl experiment.

Now consider if you will, your body. Approximately sixty percent of your body is water. So it is very important what you think about yourself, and what you think about your body. How you think can change your life. It would make no difference to me if Pastor Tracy and I were sent to Timbuktu, because with what we know, people would still find us. Thoughts can annihilate diseases, melt mountains, and pull things to you. Even satan recognizes the power of thoughts, which is why he suggests negative ideas to us, hoping we will receive them and think about them. He knows that thoughts have possibilities for evil, or for good.

If you ever receive a negative report, there is no need to panic. Just dissolve evil news with the right thoughts. The Word teaches us that, *"The thoughts of the righteous are right: but the counsels of the wicked are deceit," (Proverbs 12:5).*

There are exploits we can accomplish with our thoughts. Kingdom thoughts are our secret mind weapon! After studying the Bible for more than twenty years, I have come to the conclusion that born again believers are not normal. We are a supernatural race of beings. I am serious! Christianity is a miracle, not a religion. Many people have made Christianity into a religion, but please do not believe that. Christianity was birthed by miracles and must be sustained by miracles. Jesus brought Christianity as an earth-walk of divinity. We have been reborn into His family and He lives in us, so our thoughts must be different from those people who have not been born again. We must nurture and develop thoughts which contain hope and possibilities.

CHAPTER TEN

GRACE TO DISSOLVE MOUNTAINS

*"Forasmuch as an excellent spirit, and knowl-
edge, and understanding, interpreting of dreams,
and showing of hard sentences, and dissolving
of doubts, were found in the same Daniel, whom
the king named Belteshazzar: now let Daniel
be called, and he will show the interpretation."*
Daniel 5:12

I believe God has the answer for everything. You were once a thought from God that took shape. What happens when you put salt crystals into water? The strength of the water dissolves the crystals. I also believe the strength of good thoughts can dissolve cancer, or migraine headaches, or anything such as this that represents the curse.

This reminds me of when one of our leaders had a kidney stone. He was in agony! The doctors told him to go home to pass it. But Brother Cliff had access to a law that dissolves things.

He declared that in the Name of Jesus, he would not painfully pass that stone, he would dissolve it – and he did!

To dissolve means to melt away. If you put butter in a hot pan it melts into a fluid form. Daniel of the Bible had an anointing to dissolve problems. If Daniel possessed that grace under the old covenant, what a hope we have today. Those debts can be dissolved! Sickness can melt away! This is part of our inheritance in Christ, and the ability we have as God's divine creation.

Some folks think Christianity is just a religion. No! I would rather be in the world, serving myself, than to be in religion. Religion brings death, but Christ brings life and abundance. There is nothing or no one like Jesus. I have tried religion, but it led me into bondage and confusion. I have tried philosophies of the world, and its methods of healing the soul, but that only led me into more frustration. And when I could not help myself, Jesus came and found me. Meeting Him was the best thing that ever happened to me. Oh, how much I love Him! When no one believed in me, He did. When others were ashamed of me, He became my best Friend.

There are some young people who do not want to serve God today because they think this Jesus thing is just religion. But when young people get around the Spirit of God functioning in us, and see possibilities of how they can improve their lives and fulfill their destinies, they automatically follow Jesus.

In 2004, I was invited to preach the Gospel at a school in Zimbabwe. As I shared the reality of Christ to these precious people, the principal and many of the teachers were healed. At the end of my visit, the entire student body of two thousand students received Jesus into their hearts. Many times, when I share this story in the western world, I am met with criticism. Some ask how sincere or authentic the prayers of the students were. My response is always the same: "Well, I am glad you are not God!"

The Word says, *"Therefore He is able to save completely those who come to God through Him, because He always lives to intercede for them," (Hebrews 7:25, NIV). God is looking for people who will simply open their hearts to Him. He said, "Everyone who calls on the name of the Lord will be saved," (Romans 10:13, NIV).*

Simple, Yet Powerful

Many people think life and success have to be complicated. They have accepted the idea that simple means powerless. What they do not realize is that the things of God are very simple.

While I was preaching in Switzerland some years ago, I met a lady who was possessed by many devils, and they levitated her. Her daughter also, would somersault without touching the ground. I told her to look into my eyes, and at first she could not do it. I told her again, to look into my eyes. This time she did, and I simply told her, "You are free!" So simple! Today, she is an active member of that church, and is totally free! Sometimes people debate, "What do you mean, I am free?" But the power was in the Word I released: "You are free!"

In Haiti, I met a woman who had tumors in her breast. I told her that when I stamped my foot on the ground she would be healed, and she believed this. Other people called it stupid, and yet it worked! I am not ashamed of the Gospel!

Years ago, a sick lady came to a crusade in Canada and I wanted to put this power principle to work for her. I told her to do something she could not do before – but she refused! She was clinging to her old way of thinking. When God's grace is helping you, you cannot let your brain stop you from receiving your miracle. Only believe; think those possibility thoughts and you will win.

In the same Haitian crusade I just mentioned, there was a woman from a different city who wanted to come to the meetings, but she was unable. She decided that if she could not come to the crusade, she would just put the radio next to her chest full of tumors – and she was gloriously healed! She believed, and she had the right images in her mind. God said in His Word, He will bring to nothing the things that are; He will melt them away, using the things that are not.

"And base things of the world, and things which are despised, hath God chosen, yea, and things which are not, to bring to naught things that are." 1 Corinthians 1:28

No one can see your thoughts except God, and He will use them to bring to naught, to melt, the things that are. The Haitian woman testified that those tumors melted away. If I were to tell these stories to some people in the developed world, they would say they are crazy stories! So if these people were to try putting a radio on their chest, it would not work because their hearts are too complicated.

You must humble your heart and become like a child. Tell yourself that your heart is soft; that your heart is a miracle center where anything is possible. Doubts are destructive thoughts with negative energy attached to them. Positive thoughts have positive energy attached to them, and that energy can enter your bloodstream and go throughout your body and heal you. Thoughts have emotions; when someone has depressive thoughts it drains their energy.

Thoughts Can Melt Problems and Move Mountains

Some people ask me why I keep sharing the testimony of how my wife was healed from cancer. I do this so she can stay healthy. You overcome the enemy by the word of your testimony. Some people are too cute; God healed them and they don't talk about it anymore. But if you want to keep that healing, you need to acknowledge the Source where the healing came from. This means you have to keep talking about it.

I am saying your thoughts can create a world full of possibilities for you, or they can bring destruction to your life. Thoughts are deliberate, and you are in charge of yours. When someone speaks to you, you go home and say to yourself, "What am I going to say or think about that?" Thoughts can melt problems and move mountains. You need not be a victim of circumstances any longer. God has given you His power and Spirit, and you can change your story. You do not have to stand in line and beg any longer – you can go home to your room and change your story with your thoughts.

The doctors told us my wife had cancer that could spread all over her womb, and they said they would have to do surgery immediately. I was so nervous and the doctors were putting pressure on us. We had just started our ministry and I did not understand what was going on. So I said, "Wait, and give me a few days to think about it."

They gave us two options: one, go through the full pregnancy for the baby's sake and risk my wife's life; or two, put her on chemotherapy, but the baby might die. I said, "Dear Jesus, we are too young for this, and we are in the healing ministry!" But it does not matter who you are or what you are involved in, you have to make a choice. It makes no difference whether you are black, white, yellow or brown, the devil does not respect persons. I told the doctors, "No! I need my wife and I need my son. Either the Bible I preach from is true or it is not." We all must come to a point in our faith where we say, "Either Jesus was a liar or He is telling the truth!" And we know He was not a liar.

Allow yourself to get to a point where you say, "Jesus, I trust You. I depend upon You. I cannot go back. This is what they are saying, but I believe what You have said. My company is not going to fail! They say I have six months to live, but You said You took my sickness and You carried my disease. You said I am more than a conqueror, therefore I must and will stand firmly in agreement with what You said!" Then you have to get a hold of yourself. I remember I said within myself, "I cannot choose my son over my wife; I cannot choose my wife over my son." I said, "Jesus, I need both of them!" The Lord spoke to me. He said, "Son, whose report will you believe?"

Your Thoughts Are Your Way Out

I did not know what I was doing, but I remember listening to a teaching by brother Kenneth Copeland. He was trying to lose weight, but he just kept gaining weight. He would lose weight, but then he would gain it back, and God told him that his inner image needed to change. Until your inner image changes, nothing changes. So I wrote down, "Concerning my wife, I have to change the image of her death that was planted in my mind and the image of fear that is in my heart." (If you struggle in this area, I strongly encourage you to read Chapter One again on image and consciousness, until you have a firm grasp of this principle.) During this time, the devil tried to project thoughts to me during a miracle service. Blind eyes were being opened but he said to me, "You can heal the sick here, but I will take away the most precious thing from you."

I remember like it was yesterday – planting images in my mind of my wife healed, but then closing my eyes and seeing and hearing images of the doctor's fearsome report. I was confessing that by Jesus' stripes my wife was healed, but deep in my heart I had a different picture. I knew I was in trouble, because with my mind I had decided to say the right words, but my heart was so full of fear.

I knew I had to change my inner image of defeat and failure. How could I do that? Thoughts of God's Word can change circumstances and drive cancer out of your body. In the midst of all the bad news I decided to spend some quality time in the Word, because even though I was saying the right things, I recognized that my heart was full of fear. I went back to the Scripture not knowing what I was doing. However, now I know that the precious Holy Spirit was directing me into a divine law which God had instituted.

The heart brings forth whatever is in it, so I realized I had to change the thoughts in my heart. The way to build positive thoughts is to feed on the Word of God. So I was doing that, and I remember reading a statement by brother Kenneth Copeland. He said that the longer you keep a thought in your mind, the stronger it will be when you speak. There is a greater force behind it. When you meditate on a good thought, energy will flow through your body.

I began meditating concerning my wife, "Jesus Himself took her infirmities." And then a most amazing and precious thing happened. Jesus Himself took all the fear away that had been in my heart. God got involved! The walls in the room disappeared and I saw Jesus on the cross! Then I saw my wife's cancer on that cross, and Jesus said that He Himself took it. Now I was no longer just echoing a statement from the Bible – I was experiencing it! My thoughts had taken on shape and substance. Suddenly, all the fear had left me, and I could hardly wait to call my wife, because I knew she was healed and I was very excited! (If you have not yet read her testimony in the introduction of this book, please do so now. She tells how God marvellously healed her and she delivered a beautiful, healthy, full term baby, our precious son Joshua.) Praise be to God!

CHAPTER ELEVEN

THE HOLY SPIRIT, YOUR PARTNER IN SUCCESS

A re you aware that there is a Power available that will lead and guide you into the realm of success? That Power is a Person called the Holy Spirit. The Bible also calls Him the Power of the highest! This is the same Holy Spirit Who was working with Jesus and the prophets. He is the same Holy Spirit Who was involved in creating the universe. Now He is responsible to work with you, and to bring you to your place of rest. Think of all the exploits in the lives of all those men and women of God in the Bible. To think that this same Spirit is now working in and through me – all I can say is, Glory! Child of God, you were never supposed to struggle to fulfill your God-given purpose. You were never meant to be at the back of the line. You were designed and intended for the higher life.

Do You Know the Holy Spirit?

Every human being needs to know and experience the personal ministry of the Holy Spirit in their life. A life without the active ministry of the Holy Spirit is a life of misery. I often wonder how some people can function without Him. He is the beautiful personality in my life, and the secret behind all good things.

I love the Holy Spirit! Do you love Him? Do you know Him? Do you care to know Him? He is the secret to my joy and happiness. Everything good that we enjoy today can be attributed to the working of the Holy Spirit in our lives. My wife, children, ministry and even my very life, are all byproducts of the Holy Spirit working in me. He is the color and beauty in my life. That is why I am so excited to introduce you to Him in this chapter, as your Partner in success.

Your Partner in Success

"But the Helper, the Holy Spirit, Whom the Father will send in My name, He will teach you all things, and bring to your remembrance all things that I said to you." John 14:26 (NKJV)

We must understand and learn this about Jesus; He never exaggerates, and He never lies. His Words are full of life and truth. In our Scripture, Jesus said that the Holy Spirit would teach us all things. So there is absolutely no topic the Holy Spirit is deficient in. He knows everything! He knows everything about God, the law, science, history, business, stocks, fashion; you name it – He knows it all. The best part is, He has been assigned to teach you these things so you can win in life. *"Now we have received, not the spirit of the world, but the Spirit which is of God; that we might know the things that are freely given to us of God. Which things also we speak, not in the words which man's wisdom teacheth, but which the Holy Ghost teacheth; comparing spiritual things with spiritual," (1 Corinthians 2:12-13).*

Wow, this is so amazing! Can you imagine having a coach or mentor who knows everything about God, your future, your destiny, and your present situation? This is what the Holy Spirit is to us. He is the One Who knows everything! I know this may sound farfetched and too extravagant for the natural mind. But

I just choose to believe the Word of Jesus. Now please do not take this statement out of context. I did not say that we know all things! What I did say, is the One Who has been assigned to us as Coach, Mentor and Friend is the One Who knows all things. And that, my friend, is powerful!

His Counsel Is Perfect and His Wisdom Is Just

"I will instruct thee and teach thee in the way which thou shalt go; I will guide thee with Mine eye." Psalm 32:8

"Thus says the LORD, your Redeemer, the Holy One of Israel, I am the LORD your God, Who teaches you to profit, Who leads you in the way you should go." Isaiah 48:17 (NKJV)

Not only does the Holy Spirit teach us all things, He leads us into the realm of profit and guides us into His wealthy places. This is good news! I teach at our church the importance of cultivating a passionate relationship with the Holy Spirit. Without His active ministry in our lives, we will lack color and vigor. How some people can function without Him is beyond my comprehension! He is the beautiful fragrance in the life of a believer, and the secret behind all good things.

Who Is the Holy Spirit?

The Holy Spirit is the most intelligent Person who ever graced the face of the earth. Even Jesus, the Son of God, spoke about His reliance on the Holy Spirit. Now child of God, if Jesus, the perfect Son of God, needed the Holy Spirit to complete His Kingdom assignment, then we need Him even more. One of the most touching things I have ever discovered about the Holy Spirit is that we were created by Him. He chose our culture, the shape of our nose, the color of our eyes, and everything about our personalities. The day this truth was awakened in me was the day shame and low self-esteem died.

He Knows Everything About You

"The Spirit of God hath made me, and the breath of the Almighty hath given me life." Job 33:4

The Holy Spirit knows everything about you, and the Father has assigned Him to bring you into your place of greatness. Since He is the One Who created your personality, He knows you intimately, and your partnership with Him is of utmost importance. There are many benefits that come from having a relationship with the Holy Spirit. The one I love most is the fact that He garnishes the lives of those He helps, *"By His Spirit He hath garnished the heavens; His hand hath formed the crooked serpent," (Job 26:13).*

Webster's dictionary defines *garnish* as: to decorate, add beauty to, enhance, or raise the value of something. It also means pleasing, attractive, and impressive. I love this definition. If the Holy Spirit was responsible to garnish, or adorn the heavens, He will do the same for you, because He is not a respecter of people, places, things, or time. Whatever He will do for others, He will do for you.

I love the Holy Spirit so much – without Him I am lost, but with Him I am very dangerous! He took me on as an insecure, stammering teenager whose life was full of fear and shame, and made me a minister of the Gospel. He has taken me to many nations of the world to teach that faith in Christ is the cure for all human dysfunction. How do I know this is true? I am the proof! I was broken and He healed me.

If my dream can be realized and manifested, so can yours. If I can make it, coming from a poor village in the Caribbean, and with little education, you can make it, too! All you need is the Holy Spirit in your life. Remember, this book is about how to reprogram yourself for success. Success is how a person thinks. If your thinking is wrong, it is because your belief system is wrong. If your belief system is incorrect, your whole psychological and physical world will be off course. As the saying goes, your outer world is just a reflection of your inner world. When the Spirit is actively flowing in your life, He will guide you into the perfect knowledge that is necessary to obtain success and greatness.

Eight Things Everyone Needs To Know About the Holy Spirit

1. He guarantees our success when we partner with Him.

"...Not by might, nor by power, but by my spirit, saith the Lord of hosts." Zechariah 4:6

We cannot succeed in this life depending on our human abilities. Our natural abilities are bound to the physical senses. It is not by might (army, physical force or human strength) nor is it by power (within, or of ourselves), *"but by My Spirit, says the Lord."*

2. He is the producer of our inner successes.

"For this I labor [unto weariness], striving with all the superhuman energy which He so mightily enkindles and works within me." Colossians 1:29 (AMP)

Paul is stating here that there was something energizing him from within – there was a fire burning inside him. The word superhuman simply implies an energy superior to all human energy and strength. The supplier of that divine energy, the Holy Spirit, lives in us. This supernatural ability works in us mightily, helping us to achieve results that are beyond our physical ability. That means our potential is limitless!

3. He is our reality check.

"Howbeit when He, the Spirit of truth, is come, He will guide you into all truth: for He shall not speak of Himself; but whatsoever He shall hear, that shall He speak: and He will shew you things to come." John 16:13

Another word for truth here in the Scripture is reality. So, we can read Jesus' words as: *"Howbeit when He, the Spirit of Reality, is come, He will guide you into all reality."* The Holy Spirit is the Spirit of Reality. Too many people have a false sense of reality; a wrong perception (filtered through lies or deceived hearts) of what reality is. They think reality is whatever they can see and feel, not realizing that what they can see and feel is not everything there is – these physical senses are only temporal! When the Spirit of Reality is at work in us, our values begin to change, and life takes on a new meaning. We begin to discern more clearly what is really important, and what is not. Only the Holy Spirit can show us what reality is. Some people choose to believe the lies of the past over the brightest reality of the future.

4. He is our competitive advantage.

With the abilities of the Holy Spirit at work in us, we will never be at a disadvantage again in our lives!

"When the king of Syria was warring against Israel, after counseling with his servants, he said, In such and such a place

shall be my camp. Then the man of God sent to the king of Israel, saying, Beware that you pass not such a place, for the Syrians are coming down there. Then the king of Israel sent to the place of which [Elisha] told and warned him; and thus he protected and saved himself there repeatedly. Therefore the mind of the king of Syria was greatly troubled by this thing. He called his servants and said, Will you show me who of us is for the king of Israel? One of his servants said, None, my lord O king; but Elisha, the prophet who is in Israel, tells the king of Israel the words that you speak in your bedchamber." 2 Kings 6:8-12 (AMP)

The king of Syria kept trying to ambush the king of Israel, but was unsuccessful. Every time he laid an ambush, the prophet Elisha would send a message to the King of Israel, not to pass by that route. Time and time again, the ambush failed. In exasperation, the Syrian king called all his men together and demanded to know who the traitor was. One of his perceptive servants informed the king there was no traitor among them. Rather, the prophet Elisha could hear every secret word the king uttered in his very bedroom, and told them to the king of Israel! He could do this because the Holy Spirit, our Competitive Advantage (Who knows all things), was working with him. With the abilities of the Holy Spirit, we have the advantage over others who do not have Him.

5. He is our legal adviser. (by Tracy Weekes)

"And I will ask the Father, and He will give you another Comforter (Counselor, Helper, Intercessor, Advocate, Strengthener, and Standby), that He may remain with you forever." John 14:16 (AMP)

When we receive the Holy Spirit, He becomes our Counselor. He comes to us in the purest form of wisdom. The Bible story that I have loved since I was a child is the story of the display of Solomon's wisdom found in *1 Kings 3:16-28 (AMP)*. Solomon found himself confronted with a situation where it was difficult to determine who was telling the truth. But the faithful Adviser, the Holy Spirit, quickened him with wisdom to speak right words which would draw out the truth. He heightened Solomon's perception, enabling him to make an accurate judgment.

One definition of *counsel* is: advice or instruction given for directing the judgment or conduct of another. As a mother, I sometimes find myself in awkward situations where my kids do not always tell me the whole truth. But many times, the Holy Spirit will heighten my perceptions and quicken me to know what signs or behaviors to look for, or what words to speak to the children, which will essentially draw out the truth. This wonderful manifestation of the Spirit of God has helped me immensely.

6. He will cause you to prosper and bring you into financial profit.

Many people do not understand the financial role of the Holy Spirit. They work like slaves and still cannot meet their needs. Just one idea from the Spirit of God can bring you into much financial blessing. The Word teaches us that when the Spirit is working mightily in us, one of His many unctions is to lead us into profit. He opens doors that no man can shut. He gives us wisdom, ideas, supernatural favor, and the anointed ability to succeed, even in the days of famine.

"Thus says the LORD, your Redeemer, the Holy One of Israel, "I am the LORD your God, who teaches you to profit, Who leads you by the way you should go." Isaiah 48:17 (NKJV).

Did you know that the Holy Spirit will water your financial seed? This, my friend, is a powerful thought. I know many pastors and preachers who would never tell you this, but sowing financial seed is not enough to bring you into financial increase. Many have preached this, but it is not the full truth. It is a half truth. As a result, many of God's children are frustrated, because it seems like the seed sowing does not work. Know this; the Word always works! Please do not get discouraged and give up planting seed. Every time you plant your financial seed into the work of God, your are practicing the financial covenant; and God is eternally committed to His covenant *(Psalm 89:34)*. Every covenant has two parties, in this case, God and man. When we plant seed, God needs to bring the water, so those seeds you planted can grow and multiply.

Apply this revelation to the realm of farming. What would happen if all a farmer did was just plant seed? If he never watered his seed, it would soon die, long before it could produce the desired harvest. The same is true in the Kingdom of God; without the rain our seed will die in the ground.

"Ask ye of the Lord rain in the time of the latter rain; so the Lord shall make bright clouds, and give them showers of rain, to everyone grass in the field." Zechariah 10:1

So the Holy Spirit is called the Rain. The more of Him that is actively flowing in your life, the more He can water your seed. Next time you sow your Kingdom seed, remember to ask for and rely on the Rain, because your seed needs it to grow. The Holy Spirit will call for the financial corn and increase it in your life. Too many Christians have restricted the Holy Spirit to their own limited thinking, when God gave Him to us so that we can do more than what we think.

"And I will put My Spirit within you, and cause you to walk in My statutes, and ye shall keep My judgments, and do them. And ye shall dwell in the land that I gave to your fathers; and ye shall be My people, and I will be your God. I will also save you from all your uncleanness: and I will call for the corn, and will increase it, and lay no famine upon you." Ezekiel 36:27-29

This is wonderful! I am so happy that because of the Holy Spirit, we are not victims of circumstances. With Him working in us, we can chart our own course in God. My friend, just keep yielding yourself to Him and He will turn your life into a watered garden!

"And the Lord shall guide thee continually, and satisfy thy soul in drought, and make fat thy bones: and thou shalt be like a watered garden, and like a spring of water, whose waters fail not." Isaiah 58:11

7. He is the Master Creator.

"In the beginning God created the heaven and the earth. And the earth was without form, and void; and darkness was upon the face of the deep. And the Spirit of God moved upon the face of the waters." Genesis 1:1-2

Everything that is living was formed and created by the Holy Spirit. He is the Master Creator, and nothing can remain formless or void in His presence. He has been involved in the creation of all things, from the very beginning of Scripture to the very end. Now, He is the Creative Personality assigned to every child of God, helping us to create lives of beauty. I want you to notice in the following examples from Scripture how the Father, Son, and Holy Spirit are all mentioned within each verse.

"And the Holy Ghost descended in a bodily shape like a dove upon Him, and a voice came from Heaven, which said, Thou art my beloved Son; in Thee I am well pleased." Luke 3:22

"And Jesus, when He was baptized, went up straightway out of the water: and, lo, the heavens were opened unto Him, and he saw the Spirit of God descending like a dove, and lighting upon Him: And lo a voice from Heaven, saying, This is My beloved Son, in Whom I am well pleased." Matthew 3:16-17

"And straightway coming up out of the water, He saw the heavens opened, and the Spirit like a dove descending upon Him: And there came a voice from Heaven, saying, Thou art My beloved Son, in Whom I am well pleased. And immediately the Spirit driveth Him into the wilderness. And He was there in the wilderness forty days, tempted of Satan; and was with the wild beasts; and the angels ministered unto Him." Mark 1:10-13

In *Acts 10:38* we read, *"How God anointed Jesus of Nazareth with the Holy Ghost and with power: Who went about doing good, and healing all that were oppressed of the devil; for God was with Him."*

I love this! We see here God the Father, God the Son, and God the Holy Spirit all working together against the spirit of sickness, just as They worked together in Genesis to create the earth and everything in it. And the Holy Spirit dwells in us! If God is for us, who can be against us? It is vitally important for you to understand that the Holy Spirit is truly God, because when you were born again, He came to live in you. Whatever you allow yourself to become involved with, you are essentially inviting God to become involved in. We need to develop sensitivity to what pleases the Holy Spirit.

135

8. He is the great Revelator of truth.

"That the God of our Lord Jesus Christ, the Father of glory, may give unto you the Spirit of wisdom and revelation in the knowledge of Him: The eyes of your understanding being enlightened; that ye may know what is the hope of His calling, and what the riches of the glory of His inheritance in the saints."
Ephesians 1:17-18

The Holy Spirit is called to unfold the Kingdom of God to you. Every Kingdom secret you grasp makes you a master in that area; your insight into particular mysteries gives you authority in that realm. For example, the day I caught the revelation of my oneness with God (which is our true nature and identity), was the day I resigned from slavery to weakness, fear, sickness, and even satan himself. God can never be enslaved to the devil, therefore I can never be a slave to the devil; God and I are one. I am finished with poverty, shame, and negative emotions. The curse is no longer part of me.

Child of God, we belong to a royal family! Ours is a family of champions and conquerors, and we are with Jesus, above all principalities and powers. God has assigned His Spirit to bring us insight and revelation regarding this place where we rule by Him.

CHAPTER TWELVE

JESUS, THE GREATEST SUCCESS PHENOMENA

"Just think of Him Who endured from sinners such grievous opposition and bitter hostility against Himself [reckon up and consider it all in comparison with your trials], so that you may not grow weary or exhausted, losing heart and relaxing and fainting in your minds." Hebrews 12:3 (AMP)

I was so excited when the Holy Spirit dropped these words into my heart: Jesus, the greatest success Phenomena! I want to bring out in this chapter the humanity of Christ. He encountered incredible negativity, yet He rose above it all to become the greatest success Phenomena. After two thousand years we are still talking about His impact. As I mentioned in a previous chapter, success is more than words. Success encompasses:

- your way of thinking.
- your ideas.
- the things you do.
- the words you speak.
- how you influence those around you to think like you &
- how you inspire others to make a positive impact in the world.

Success also means influencing others to become their best, with the conviction to die for what you believe, if need be. No one knows this better than Jesus Himself. I like what the Word says concerning Jesus: *"But God demonstrates His own love toward us, in that while we were still sinners, Christ died for us," (Romans 5:8, NKJV).*

"A man who does not have something for which
he is willing to die is not fit to live."
— Martin Luther King Jr.

When I take a clear look at the life of Jesus, I can say with conviction that He was an extraordinary success, and He proved this by the great value He has bestowed upon us.

"Very rarely will anyone die for a righteous person, though for a good person someone might possibly dare to die. But God demonstrates His own love for us in this: While we were still sinners, Christ died for us." Romans 5:7-8 (NIV)

Jesus' Success Is Your Story

Over the years religion has portrayed this Prince from Nazareth as a weak, poor, person. My intention in this chapter is to debunk that ideology concerning the Prince of Life, *(see Acts 3:15, KJV).* Yes indeed, Jesus went through hell, but He came out triumphantly. Every challenge He faced as a man, He always found a way out. No man born of a woman has ever faced the mental hostility He faced, yet He still rose to become the greatest icon Who ever lived. *Hebrews 12:3 (AMP)* tells us, *"Just think of Him, Who endured from sinners such grievous opposition and bitter hostility against Himself."*

What was the grievous opposition and bitter hostility? We know He suffered on the cross, but His suffering and rejection did not start at the cross; He endured these things all His life. We need to understand that Jesus was not only God in the flesh, He was also a man. As a man, He had emotions and feelings like we do. He had to overcome the pain of rejection and all kinds of temptation. Throughout His life and ministry, He always rose above the pressures and unfriendly scrutiny to manifest the qualities of great leadership and success.

Jesus Succeeded and Won at Everything

Do you know that Jesus was a success in everything He did? You may not have thought of this before. Remember, Jesus did not operate as God, yet everything He did was off the charts.

Let us look first at His birth. He had to rise above the criticism and the naysayers concerning the controversy of His birth, which in the mindset of Jewish culture at that time, was very shameful. Over sixty times, Jesus had to remind the Jews that God was indeed His Father. The question we need to ask ourselves is, "Why?" We as believers today know that His birth was supernatural – that God indeed is His Father. but this was not the consensus of everyone in Bethlehem or Nazareth. A large portion of the people did not believe this supernatural story about a virgin giving birth. For them, Jesus' birth was the result of plain old fornication, and no one knew who His actual father was. This made Him an outcast in their society.

In spite of tremendous opposition, Jesus rose rapidly above it all to become the greatest Man and Leader Who ever lived. Over the years, I have met so many people who have become prisoners of their past. They just could not let go of the hurts from yesterday. But we see Jesus rising above all the odds, and winning triumphantly!

Six Reasons Why Jesus Was So Successful

1. He never connected Himself with His natural roots.

Jesus was more aware of His spiritual connection than His biological roots.

Jesus was very certain of His identity, and this is something we all need to learn from. He knew God was His father, and He drew from God His identity and divine purpose. Every young Jewish boy draws his identity and dignity from his father, and Jesus was no different. He knew His Father was from Heaven.

Please do not misunderstand me, I love my natural roots! In the last few years we have seen a large number of Caribbean people coming to our church, and we love it! I love my island people, and when we enjoy our food fellowships, all Heaven comes into the room, Glory! I love my island food ... my jerk chicken and my salt fish etc. ... I am getting hungry now! However, my point is that whatever roots you may come from, you should love it, but not at the expense of your true roots. Jesus chose the spiritual over the natural, and it was one of the keys to His great success. This is what He said, *"For I came down from Heaven, not to do Mine own will, but the will of Him that sent me," (John 6:38).*

Jesus also said, *"My Father, Who has given them to Me, is greater than all; and no one is able to snatch them out of My Father's hand. I and My Father are one," (John 10:29-30, NKJV).* Now that is powerful! Can you imagine how outrageous the Jews considered His statement to be, but Jesus never allowed their limited revelation to stop Him from moving forward. He knew God was His Father, and that was all that mattered.

"And now come I to Thee; and these things I speak in the world, that they might have my joy fulfilled in themselves. I have given them Thy word; and the world hath hated them, because they are not of the world, even as I am not of the world. I pray not that Thou shouldest take them out of the world, but that thou shouldest keep them from the evil. They are not of the world, even as I am not of the world. Sanctify them through Thy truth: Thy word is truth. As Thou hast sent Me into the world, even so have I also sent them into the world. And for their sakes I sanctify Myself, that they also might be sanctified through the truth." John 17:13-19

Wow! Look at that! *John 17:1-20* should be your personal prayer over your family, your church, and those you have been given authority over in the spirit.

2. He mastered the art of living above the sting of rejection and cynicism.

Failure to accomplish this has been the downfall of many people. There is a saying in the Caribbean that says, "If you cannot stand the heat, stay out of the kitchen!" Many people have given up on their dreams because of a little pressure. My friend, pressure comes, not to destroy you, but to solidify the dream that is within you. Every dream must pass the tests of pressure and criticism to secure its authenticity.

Every time Jesus experienced rejection and cynicism, He always rose up and dominated them with the force of love. If you and I desire to win in life, we will do very well to follow Jesus' example. Some of Jesus' greatest critics were the Pharisees. This is what they said: *"...This fellow doth not cast out devils, but by beelzebub the prince of the devils. And Jesus knew their thoughts, and said unto them, Every kingdom divided against itself is brought to desolation; and every city or house divided against itself shall not stand: And if satan cast out satan, he is divided against himself; how shall then his kingdom stand? And if I by beelzebub cast out devils, by whom do your children cast them out? Therefore they shall be your judges. But if I cast out devils by the Spirit of God, then the Kingdom of God is come unto you," (Matthew 12:24-28).*

Now let us bring this statement into today's language. *"This fellow does not cast out demons except by beelzebub, the ruler of the demons."* What the Pharisees were saying here is that Jesus' success was not authentic because He used sorcery to influence people. Can you imagine if there was a rumor going around your town that you were using witchcraft to advance your business practice? This would not sit well with most people. This is what Jesus had to face every time He functioned in His calling. Yet He always won.

3. He had a superior mindset to rise above His challenges and to subdue all negative forces.

Look at the mental attitude of Jesus: *"And there arose a great storm of wind, and the waves beat into the ship, so that it was now full. And He was in the hinder part of the ship, asleep on a pillow: and they awoke Him, and say unto Him, Master, carest thou not that we perish? And He arose, and rebuked the wind, and said unto the sea, Peace, be still. And the wind ceased, and there was a great calm. And He said unto them, Why are ye so fearful? How is it that ye have no faith? And they feared exceedingly, and said one to another, What manner of man is this, that even the wind and the sea obey Him?" Mark 4:37-41*

Here again, we see that Jesus refused to bow to the demon of negativity and sense knowledge. My friend, this is the same mindset we need to possess if we desire to win in life. We are not called to *'freak out'* over every sign of bad news, or any negativity that comes our way. Here is an example of a Man who was tested by life's circumstances, yet He remained calm and won the victory over them. We are told that in the middle of a storm He was sleeping. Who sleeps in the middle of a storm? A man who is in charge of his environment. The Amplified Bible tells us that the storm was of hurricane proportions. The waves coming into the boat were ten to fifteen feet high. In the midst of this, Jesus was sleeping.

What kind of mind and attitude was this? The mind of a Conqueror. Every time negative forces tried to detour Jesus from His mission, He always remained faithful to the tested and proven Words of His Father. Today, He is calling us as believers to develop that same confidence in our Heavenly Father's Word. In a world filled with pride, doubt and sense knowledge, God is looking for believers who will manifest this Christ-like attitude during every testing and storm.

I can say with absolute confidence, that if you look closely at the success of every person who has overcome negativity and won, you will see that they have followed the tested and proven success principles of Jesus, even though some are too prideful to admit it.

4. He understood and practiced the Law of Consistency and Focus

Focus brings energy and power.

"Therefore we also, since we are surrounded by so great a cloud of witnesses, let us lay aside every weight, and the sin which so easily ensnares us, and let us run with endurance the race that is set before us, looking unto Jesus, the Author and Finisher of our faith, Who for the joy that was set before Him endured the cross, despising the shame, and has sat down at the right hand

of the throne of God. For consider Him who endured such hostility from sinners against Himself, lest you become weary and discouraged in your souls." Hebrews 12:1-3 (NKJV)

The only reason a man fails in life is broken focus. Focus brings energy and power to almost anything you do in life, whether it is physical or mental. If you desire to make progress in any area, learning this principle is a must. Jesus proved this principle. His life exemplified consistency and focus. From His childhood until His death, He remained focused on His Father's Word and mission.

The Razor Sharp Mind of Jesus

When Jesus walked on earth, great multitudes came to Him with their sick. Among them were the lame, blind, dumb and maimed, and Jesus healed them all! One of the outstanding characteristics I love most about Jesus was His ability to stay focused in the middle of life challenges. As I said before, Jesus had the mind of a conqueror. His concentration was razor sharp. With His thoughts and faith, He even postponed His own death.

In *Luke 22:44 (AMP)* we read the account of Jesus' great mental agony, *"And being in an agony (of mind), He prayed (all the) more earnestly and intently, and His sweat became like great clots of blood dropping down upon the ground."* He was destined to die on the cross, but satan tried to kill Him prematurely. Can you imagine Jesus' mental distress at anticipating the cross? With the power of focus He prevailed over the temptation to avoid it. My friend, anyone can start out doing great things in life, but the only ones who win are those who finish the race. Focus plays a great role in winning the prize.

Five Things Jesus Taught Me About the Power of Focus

- Focus releases power and energy for you to fulfill your assignment. Jesus told His disciples to wait for the Spirit.
- Focus brings uncommon clarity that causes you to stay true to your mission, (see *Matthew 10:5-15*).
- Focus brings growth into areas where there is weakness. It is not possible for you to concentrate on your positive goals and not grow.
- Focus can assist in reducing the harmful effects linked to tension and stress on your body.
- Focus releases creativity. Some of the most creative people are focus driven, and Jesus is the Master of them all.

5. He never tried to succeed alone.

This is a problem for most people in the world; they struggle with this disease. Everybody wants to be the big-shot. No one wants to have a mentor. Jesus had a different mindset from the world and that is why He won every time. Those who choose to walk in His footsteps will also win like Him.

"I can of Myself do nothing. As I hear, I judge; and My judgment is righteous, because I do not seek My own will but the will of the Father who sent Me." John 5:30 (NKJV)

No man is an island. You need people, and you need God if you are going to make it in life. Whether you enjoy hearing this or not, the truth is that our lives are interconnected. Everything you have today is directly connected with people! Success is a collection of relationships. Without a client, a lawyer has no career. Without a patient, a doctor has no practice. Your future is connected to people around you; no one obtains success alone.

Your success is also someone else' success. Jesus understood this very well. That is the reason He never chose to win alone.

6. He understood the power of words.

Jesus was a Master of words. With His words He ruled and dominated His world. As I often say, words are more than sound! No one understood this better than Jesus. All throughout His ministry, He used the power of words to frame His world for success. Jesus turned water into wine, opened blind eyes, and brought the dead back to life. On one occasion, His disciples fished all night and could not catch anything. When Jesus saw they were unsuccessful, He helped them by saying, *"Throw your net on the right side of the boat and you will find some," (John 21:6, NIV).* When they did, they were unable to haul the net in because of the large number of fish. Wow!

I want you to pay close attention to Jesus' words. He said, *"Throw your net on the right side of the boat and you will find some."* If there was one place in all the water where the disciples were not expecting to find any fish, it was definitely around their ship, as they had troubled that spot all night long. The fish ought to have fled from there. The Bible says that when the disciples followed Jesus' instructions, they were unable to haul the net in because of the large number of fish. The big question is, where did those fish come from? I will tell you where; they came from the words of Jesus. Throughout His ministry, Jesus used His words to frame His world with success. My friend, you can also do the same. Remember, Jesus is the same yesterday, today and forever. Everything He can do, you can do also. He is just waiting for you to speak, so He can move on your behalf.

CHAPTER THIRTEEN

DECLARING YOUR SUCCESS

"Thou shalt also decree a thing, and it shall be established unto thee: and the light shall shine upon thy ways." Job 22:28

Do you know that the spoken words of yesterday are the harvested fields of today? Every success or failure in your life today is the result of what you either have or have not sown yesterday. Some have made the mistake of saying nothing, and just like an uncultivated garden, they received a harvest of weeds. Weeds come as a result of the curse. Weeds can come in the form of sickness, fear, lack and depression. No one needs to plant weeds – they just come! So if we want to reap a harvest of health, faith, abundance and joy, we need to plant word gardens in line with our desires.

Planning for Your Harvest and Killing the Weeds

One of the ways we can reprogram ourselves for success is to reprogram our mouths. Many people fail in life because their declarations are not consistent with God's success plan for their lives. You cannot expect to reap success when you are talking failure. Success is the result of positive faith declarations. Your mouth is for more than eating! The Scripture tells us that, *"Death and life are in the power of the tongue," (Proverbs*

18:21). With your tongue you can be a blessing, or with your tongue you can curse your future.

Your mouth is intended to be a blessing center. We could say that your tongue is designed to be a springboard that launches blessings into your life, as well as the lives of others. You can use your mouth to chart your course in life, open new doors, and create amazing opportunities.

Everything Pastor Tracy and I have in our personal lives and ministry has come about this way. We take the Word of God and fight with it. Yes, satan is defeated, but sometimes we have to remind him about that fact! Actually, we have discovered that most of the time we are not even dealing with an evil spirit, but rather a negative, stubborn atmosphere that is not consistent with our dreams.

You Can Change Anything With the Word of God

There is no situation that cannot be altered with the Word of God. The Word of God is a prophetic package carrying His blessings. It has been tested to the utmost and proven very reliable. God used His Word to build the entire universe. Child of God, think about that for moment! The Words of God that you are privileged to speak were used by Him to create the galaxies and heavens. The Bible says, *"Let us hold fast the profession of our faith without wavering; for He is faithful that promised,"* *(Hebrews 10:23).*

During Jesus' time on earth, He was very successful in everything He set out to do, because He always spoke the Word of God. Jesus spoke to fever, deaf ears, missing limbs and blind eyes, and they all obeyed Him. Most people would laugh at the idea that a fever can hear, or a missing limb can appear. In Jesus' ministry, these things clearly did happen.

"And great multitudes came unto Him, having with them those that were lame, blind, dumb, maimed, and many others, and cast them down at Jesus' feet; and He healed them: Insomuch that the multitude wondered, when they saw the dumb to speak, the maimed to be whole, the lame to walk, and the blind to see: and they glorified the God of Israel." Matthew 15:30-31

People were immediately made whole after Jesus spoke to them. A Roman centurion recognized this and released great faith in Jesus' spoken Word for the healing of his servant, *"The centurion answered and said, Lord, I am not worthy that thou shouldest come under my roof: but speak the word only, and my servant shall be healed," (Matthew 8:8).*

On another occasion, Jesus spoke to the natural elements of earth and they obeyed Him.

"And, behold, there arose a great tempest in the sea, insomuch that the ship was covered with the waves: but He was asleep. And His disciples came to Him, and awoke Him, saying, Lord, save us: we perish. And He saith unto them, Why are ye fearful, O ye of little faith? Then He arose, and rebuked the winds and the sea; and there was a great calm. But the men marveled, saying, What manner of man is this, that even the winds and the sea obey Him!" Matthew 8:24-27

What Was Jesus' Secret?

Jesus' secret weapon was the Word of His Father within Him. Every time Jesus spoke, He was always conscious of His Father Who was in Him.

"For I have not spoken of Myself; but the Father which sent Me, He gave me a commandment, what I should say, and what I should speak. And I know that His commandment is life

everlasting: whatsoever I speak therefore, even as the Father said unto Me, so I speak." John 12:49-50

Jesus never depended on Himself, but was always attentive to the wisdom of His Father in every situation He faced. We can learn from Him, and imitate His example.

"Most assuredly, I say to you, the Son can do nothing of Himself, but what He sees the Father do; for whatever He does, the Son also does in like manner." John 5:19 (NKJV)

The Father in you is now, watching over the words you speak, to bring them to pass, just like He did for Jesus. He loves you the same way He loves Jesus – nothing less, nothing more. He will do everything necessary to bring those words to pass. Therefore, open your mouth and declare His promises over your life. By doing this, you can open new doors, uncommon opportunities, and covenant relationships. With the Word of God in your mouth, you can do anything that God can do.

In 2004 the Lord spoke to me, "Take My Gospel to the nation of Brazil." At that time, I had no contacts in Brazil. God simply told me to use my mouth and open that door. We started the process by decreeing that, "The nation of Brazil is open to us for the Gospel," and that is exactly what happened. Contacts came forward and doors opened. Today that nation is wide open for us to preach the Gospel.

I remember another time when we needed $50,000 in three days for a down payment on our house. All we had was $10,000 in the bank. Again, the Lord spoke to me saying, "If you take care of My house, I will take care of your house."

Those words pierced my heart and I wept like a baby. The following day, I went to the bank and withdrew all my life savings and invested it in the work of God. His Words were resounding within me, **"If you take care of My house, I will take care of your house."** Two days later, all the money came in to put the down payment on that house. God moved on the hearts of a wonderful couple to help us with the money. Today, they are a Boaz to my ministry, and to Pastor Tracy and I personally.

Child of God, the principles in this book work best when you use them, not just read them! I habitually practice them, and I am one hundred percent convinced that if you practice these principles, your life will never be the same!

Speak Yourself into Success and Blessings

"For with the heart man believeth unto righteousness; and with the mouth confession is made unto salvation." Romans 10:10

Every time you believe the Word of God, you are blessed, but for you to see change in your life, you have to speak. The Word says that confession brings you into salvation. That word salvation in Romans chapter ten comes from the Greek word sózó, which means to be healed, saved, protected, provided for and made whole. It also means to have nothing missing or broken in your life.

There is no redemptive blessing available to you without a positive faith confession. This is where many of God's children miss out. In the book of Mark, Jesus reveals this same powerful principle linking success with speaking. He says, *"For verily I say unto you, That whosoever shall say unto this mountain, Be thou removed, and be thou cast into the sea; and shall not doubt in his heart, but shall believe that those things which he saith shall come to pass; he shall have whatsoever he saith.*

Therefore I say unto you, What things soever ye desire, when ye pray, believe that ye receive them, and ye shall have them," *(Mark 11:23-24).*

So you see, just believing is not enough. What you are speaking, and how often you are speaking, is of paramount importance. You may not have seen your breakthrough yet, but please, please do not stop talking! Many believe, but only a few people speak, and in the speaking is where salvation comes.

Provision and Nourishment Are in Your Mouth

"A man's belly shall be satisfied with the fruit of his mouth; and with the increase of his lips shall he be filled. Death and life are in the power of the tongue: and they that love it shall eat the fruit thereof." Proverbs 18 :20-21.

God has programmed your tongue with power. Your tongue can harm you, bring you down, or even destroy the works of your hands. But there is also a unique power built inside your tongue that can bring you much provision.

"A man shall be satisfied with good by the fruit of his mouth." Proverbs 12:14

The word fruit here means provision and nourishment. So we see, there is provision and nourishment in your mouth, or in the words you choose to speak. As you speak the Word of God into the atmosphere, God's Spirit will provide what has been missing in your life.

God Will Establish What You Speak

Perhaps you are included in the vast number of people who have asked the questions:

"How can I become who I want to be?"
"How do I go where I want to go?"
"How do I make all my dreams and prophecies come to pass?"

The answers to these very important questions are found in *2 Thessalonians 2:16-17: "Now our Lord Jesus Christ Himself, and God, even our Father, which hath loved us, and hath given us everlasting consolation and good hope through grace, Comfort your hearts, and stablish you in every good word and work."* The word *establish* means: to set up; to be found, to bring about, generate, and put into a favorable position. This is good news!

Our verse says the *"Lord Jesus Christ Himself ...stablish you in every good word and work."* Jesus Himself is responsible to set up, generate, build, bring into being, validate and put you into a favorable position. How does He do it? Through your faith declarations. Every time you declare a good word, or do a good work that is based on your redemption, Jesus Himself will establish that in your life. This, my friend, is good news!

"Seeing then that we have a great high priest, that is passed into the heavens, Jesus the Son of God, let us hold fast our profession." Hebrews 4:14

It is time for you to begin speaking boldly, so the Lord Himself can establish you in all the success and blessing He has ordained for you. As you speak with this insight, your words will carry greater weight in the spirit than before, as well as on earth. At this level of revelation knowledge, you can speak yourself into success and blessings faster than those who do not know this principle. Open your mouth wide, so God can establish your words and deeds!

Taking Jesus Public

After you have put Jesus' Words in your heart, than you have to take Him public. This means you must declare what you believe. Some may call you crazy, but do not be dismayed; that just goes with the territory of belonging to the family of champions! Welcome! Look at the exploits of your family:

- Abraham declared that he was a father of many nations, even before his wife conceived his child. He did not consider the fact that he was one hundred years old, or the fact that his ninety year old wife had been barren all her life and was now past childbearing age. He believed what God had spoken to him was true.
- Jesus declared that He was the Son of God, and the grave could not hold Him!
- Moses declared to Pharaoh that I AM sent him to deliver His people.
- Joseph declared his dreams to all who cared to listen. One day, his dreams became a reality, and he saved a nation from famine.

Your Mouth Is Your Way Out of Trouble

"Whoso keepeth his mouth and his tongue keepeth his soul from troubles." Proverbs 21:23

There is tremendous power in your mouth. All you have to do is boldly declare your desires. Your mouth is your way out of trouble. Please do not just read these things – practice them! There might be people at this very moment who are speaking evil and cursed things against you. Some may have even vowed to cover your environment with negativity and hardship. So wake up, take charge, and do something about it! Now is not time for you to be silent! Your environment needs to be cleaned with your faith declarations. The worst thing you can do is to keep quiet. Resolve that you are going to say what God says about you. Resolve that you are going to have talking sessions. Before we go any further, let us begin right now. Boldly say these declarations out loud:

Power Talk for Your Day

"I release the forces of life that will attract unto me this day the finances, material substances, right relationships and everything I need to fulfill my God-given destiny! Father, I thank You for the power of Your Word which causes me to function from a place of rest and mastery over all situations. I live victoriously over all the destructive elements of this world, in the Name of Jesus! I refuse to struggle for anything, because all things are mine! I am possessor of all things, because I am the seed of Abraham. My faith is producing results for me today as I act on this Word! I am walking in the reality of who I am in Christ. I am an heir of God, and a joint heir with Christ. I boldly declare this is my identity! This is who I am."

A few years ago, I was listening to a sermon by a minister who I love dearly. He said that when his ministry was quite small, he drove to a large soccer stadium in his city and said, "One day, I will hold a church service in that place!"

Everyone said, "Come on Pastor, our church is too small for that!" However, the Holy Ghost told that minister that if he would talk, the Spirit Himself would cause his words to travel and find ears. So he started talking, "I will have my church at the stadium!"

The result? God confirmed his words and he had a service in that same stadium with one million people in attendance! He had big screen televisions all over the grounds just to accommodate the overflow from the stadium. God is no respecter of persons, places, or time. If He can establish the faith declarations of that minister, He can do the same for you with regard to your dreams.

Begin today to create your future by speaking. Set some goals and start to prophesy. They can be business goals, financial goals, or personal goals. Just set some goals and give your words a purpose. Until you speak, your enemies remain in charge! So take charge now, and let your life bring honor and glory to God!

CHAPTER FOURTEEN

THE PSYCHOLOGY OF WINNING

"Winning is not a sometime thing; it's an all the time thing. You don't win once in a while; you don't do things right once in a while; you do them right all of the time. Winning is a habit. Unfortunately, so is losing." Vince Lombardi

Veteran football coach Vince Lombardi once said, "Winning is everything." Vince Lombardi was one of America's greatest football coaches, who enjoyed much success during his career. He trained his team to do just one thing in every game: win! He believed that failure was not an option, and knew that second place would not get the prize. Only the winning team takes home the gold.

The Kingdom of Heaven is similar in this regard. God has called us to win at all times. Partial failure is really failure altogether. In Christ, our divine nature is that we are more than conquerors, which means we are victorious every time. God is glorified and happy when He sees His children triumphant!

"Now thanks be unto God, which always causeth us to triumph in Christ, and maketh manifest the savour of His knowledge by us in every place. For we are unto God a sweet savour of Christ, in them that are saved, and in them that perish." 2 Corinthians 2:14-15

"What shall we then say to these things? If God be for us, who can be against us? He that spared not His own Son, but delivered Him up for us all, how shall He not with Him also freely give us all things? Who shall lay any thing to the charge of God's elect? It is God that justifieth. Who is he that condemneth? It is Christ that died, yea rather, that is risen again, Who is even at the right hand of God, Who also maketh intercession for us. Who shall separate us from the love of Christ? Shall tribulation, or distress, or persecution, or famine, or nakedness, or peril, or sword? As it is written, For Thy sake we are killed all the day long; we are accounted as sheep for the slaughter. Nay, in all these things we are more than conquerors through Him that loved us. For I am persuaded, that neither death, nor life, nor angels, nor principalities, nor powers, nor things present, nor things to come, Nor height, nor depth, nor any other creature, shall be able to separate us from the love of God, which is in Christ Jesus our Lord." Romans 8:31-39

I have to tell you, winning is not an accidental event. No one wins by chance. Winning does not grow wings and fly into your hands just because you are a child of the Kingdom. Success comes to those who desire it, work for it and practice the principles that make it happen. Winning is a similar mindset. You could call it the way of winning, and it is the way of the Kingdom of God. He desires every child born into His family to live the winning lifestyle. God sees you winning in absolutely every area of your life: finances, marriage, business, ministry, and everything you set your hands to do. Winning is your divine inheritance.

"For whatsoever is born of God overcometh the world: and this is the victory that overcometh the world, even our faith." 1 John 5:4

"Ye are of God, little children, and have overcome them: because greater is He that is in you, than he that is in the world." 1 John 4:4

Psychology of Winning

What is the psychology of winning? How does it relate to reprogramming ourselves for success? I am glad you are asking these very important questions. In this chapter, I will be answering both.

In my personal view, the psychology of winning is having the mindset that you win every time; you never even consider failure as an option. Child of God, you can develop this kind of mindset.

"For as he thinketh in his heart, so is he." Proverbs 23:7

The psychology of winning is the way Jesus Christ our Lord taught us to live every day. He said that He came to give us life more abundantly; a life of no begging, no fear, no lack, no shame and no anxiety. This is exactly how Jesus lived when He was on earth. He modeled winning for us the entire time He walked this earth in the flesh. The demons who tried to devise His failure trembled, and cried out for help when Jesus came on the scene. See *Matthew 8:28-32.*

Jesus Is a Winner

Jesus exercised total dominion over all powers of the air, land and sea, and He wants you to follow His example. He wants you to be a success!

Success Is About Winning

You should appreciate any useful, practical information that will help you to win in life and reach your highest calling. In his book *The Psychology of Winning*, Dr. Denis Waitley details the steps to winning. These steps are used extensively by both Olympic athletes and top business executives. Dr. Waitley speaks of applying the *law of self-expectancy*, whereby you can easily and quickly boost your own winning average. Self-expectation, or the power of your desire, is an attitude that all winners possess.

Too many people are living far below their fullest potential. God has placed seeds of destiny in your heart for the life and future He planned for you. He wants you to desire those things that align with your life vision, which is the purpose for which you were born.

"Blessed is the man that walketh not in the counsel of the ungodly, nor standeth in the way of sinners, nor sitteth in the seat of the scornful. But his delight is in the law of the Lord; and in His law doth he meditate day and night. And he shall be like a tree planted by the rivers of water, that bringeth forth his fruit in his season; his leaf also shall not wither; and whatsoever he doeth shall prosper." Psalm 1:1-3

God has made provision for every Christian to live in complete victory in every area of their lives. In *1 Corinthians 15:57*, we see that our victory is already established: *"But thanks be to God which giveth us the victory through our Lord Jesus Christ."* We do not have to merit the victory. Our victory has already been purchased and provided for us! All we have to do is accept what Jesus has already done.

The Power of Your Desire

In the school of winning, the power of your desire is of utmost importance. Desire plays a vital role in our ability to achieve more in this life. We must have a strong desire for success. I have seen people fail in life, and in business, because their desire for success was not stronger than the problems they faced. They just gave up when they encountered challenges. However, when your desire for success is strong, you view those challenges as stepping stones to your success. People with a weak desire generally do not achieve much in life. They easily settle for the status quo. Sometimes they are afraid to obey God, try a new venture, take a risk, start a business, make an investment, or travel to an unfamiliar place. You have to make a decision to desire the success God wants for you.

Life's trials and challenges are often tough, and only the tough-minded can sail through. A strong desire will enable us to persevere through the obstacles. People with strong desires are passionate, know what they want in life, and go after it.

Paul the apostle and King David are great examples of people from the Bible who had strong desires. Apostle Paul was very passionate about knowing the Lord Jesus Christ. That was his only desire. He literally left all he had in order to know Christ. David, a shepherd boy called to be king over Israel, wrote about his heart's desire for God: *"As the deer pants for the water brooks, so pants my soul for You, O God. My soul thirsts for God, for the living God,"* *(Psalm 42:1-2b, NKJV).*

God's divine plan for you is to have an abundant life. Consequently, that should be your desire. Allow yourself to dream again as you are reading the pages of this book. Begin to reprogram your life for success. Let your heart's desires line up with the Word of God, and His plans and purposes for your life. To be truly successful, we simply must surrender our desires to God.

"Delight yourself also in the Lord, and He shall give you the desires of your heart." Psalm 37:4 (NKJV)

If You Can See it, You Can Have It

"And the LORD said unto Abram, after that Lot was separated from him, Lift up now thine eyes, and look from the place where thou art northward, and southward, and eastward, and westward: For all the land which thou seest, to thee will I give it, and to thy seed for ever. And I will make thy seed as the dust of the earth: so that if a man can number the dust of the earth, then shall thy seed also be numbered. Arise, walk through the land in the length of it and in the breadth of it; for I will give it unto thee." Genesis 13:14-17

That is what God is saying to you today. As far as your eyes can see, it is yours! So what can you see? Many of God's children have struggled to enter into their God-given inheritance because they have had no workable knowledge of the *laws of sight*. Many claim they cannot see, and those who see, often see the wrong picture. I pray that as you keep reading this book, your eyes will be opened to see the wonders of God.

The Law of Sight

Seeing is a vital Kingdom law. This is what empowered Abraham's faith. The *law of sight* says, "What you see in your heart and mind is what you will get in natural reality." If you can see something in your heart, you will see it in your path. God told Abraham that as far as his eyes could see, He would give it to him. And because God is no respecter of persons, times or seasons, He is saying the same thing to you today! How far can you see?

162

Can you see your ministry growing? Can you see your loved ones saved and delivered from satan's deceptive grip? Can you see your physical body healed, and your finances increased and multiplied for the Kingdom of God? Can you see God using you to bring healing to your world? Until you see it, you will never speak. Until you see it, God will not authorize it.

Before Pastor Tracy and I started this wonderful ministry, we spent hours seeing and meditating on the visions and dreams in our hearts and minds. Today, the vision is speaking louder and louder. We have taken the Gospel to many nations of the world. The blind see, the deaf hear, the crippled walk, churches and Bible Training Centers have been established, and thousands of people have been saved and transformed by the glorious Gospel. Only Heaven knows all that has taken place! All this started when we habitually studied and began to see the Scriptures and the visions coming into place in our lives. The great thing about all of this is that we are just getting started. We still have many more dreams to be birthed. So, join us on this spiritual journey, as we learn how to see into the realm of possibility!

How Do You See?

"While we look not at the things which are seen, but at the things which are not seen: for the things which are seen are temporal; but the things which are not seen are eternal."
2 Corinthians 4:18

This has been the question of the ages, yet the answer is so simple. You see with your redemptive mind and thoughts. I always say that the mind of a believer is different from the mind of someone who is not saved. The Word teaches that we are partakers of His grace, *"And of His fullness have all we received, and grace for grace,"* *(John 1:16)*. We are complete in Him.

Never look at the facts in your life, for they are not real. The only true reality is the Word of God. Jesus, in His priestly prayer to His Father said, *"Thy Word is Truth!" (John 17:17).* This means that the Word of God is reality. Anything outside of His Word is not reality. Sickness, lack, disease, failure, low self-esteem and inferiority are just disfigured shadows. They are mirages compared to the Word of God.

I urge you to look, dream, and meditate on the Word of God, so that the Word of God can deliver your inheritance to you. In the realm of the spirit, the application of these laws determine your success. The pure and righteous thoughts which come to your mind are inspired by the Holy Spirit. They are actually the visions of God for your life. I hope you caught that! When you believe the visions, they become substance in the spirit realm. Then, when you speak, they become realities in the earth. If you can see it in your mind and heart, you will have it!

Visualization Principles

1. Learn to see, in your mind's eye, the vision you received from the Word of God coming to pass (*Genesis 13:14-17*).

2. All spiritual visions come from Holy Spirit, and are manifested on the screen of your renewed mind (*1 Corinthians 2:10*).

3. The renewed mind is a friend of Jehovah (*Romans 8:6b*).

4. Your renewed mind is the key to walking in the supernatural (*Romans 12:1-3; Isaiah 26:3*).

5. Your mind is the doorway to the spirit, so please use it for God! (*Romans 8:5-7; Colossians 3:1-2*).

THE POWER OF YOUR GIFT

"The greatest thing you can do for yourself is to take the time to discover why you were born, and discover the gifts and talents you were endowed with." Everton Weekes

Have you ever found yourself in what seemed like an impossible situation? Or like my Dad used to say, *between a rock and a hard place*? Have you been praying and seeking God for a way out of that difficult predicament you find yourself in? I think we all have done that, but I want you to know that God has already provided a solution to the situation you are facing. God is well aware of every challenge you will ever face. He sees your setbacks, and He has already equipped you with the strategies and wisdom necessary for your success. These abilities are called your gifts.

Are you able to identify the gifts and talents God has given to you? They are very important to both you and God, and He wants you to recognize all the abilities you have received from Him. The desire of my heart is to help you open your mind so that you may recognize your God-given gifts. He intends for you to enjoy success, and that success is linked to the gifts and talents He has already put inside you. The unfolding and developing of your gifts will cause your destiny to manifest. Every talent you have is divine confirmation of God's plan to bless you.

"This book of the law shall not depart out of thy mouth; but thou shalt meditate therein day and night, that thou mayest observe to do according to all that is written therein: for then thou shalt make thy way prosperous, and then thou shalt have good success." Joshua 1:8

You will make your way prosperous! Not God – you! You make your own way prosperous by utilizing the kingdom gifts and talents God has given you.

How to Locate Your Gift

Have you ever taken time to examine your gift? In this chapter, I will share some thoughts that may help you to look at your gift differently. These ideas have helped me, and thousands of others, to find their sweet spot. Everyone was born with a gift, but like hinges on a door, most gifts are overlooked. Think about this for a moment. Have you ever walked up to a door and said, "These hinges are so beautiful!" No one does, because the hinges are hidden. They are not obvious to the eye. But what happens if there are no hinges? The door is useless, because every door, whether big or small, requires hinges to open and close. The same concept applies to your gifts; they are like hinges that open big doors to your destiny.

Proverbs 18:16 says, "A man's gift maketh room for him, and bringeth him before great men." The phrase *maketh room* refers to removing obstacles and clearing things out of the way. This is similar to what David said concerning his enemy, *"...Then David said, God hath broken in upon mine enemies by mine hand like the breaking forth of waters," (1 Chronicles 14:11b).*

I like that! Being born in the Caribbean, I think I have a little understanding of what David is saying here. I have seen waters bursting forth into my little village countless times. I have seen cars, buses and houses become floating objects when the flood broke forth. There were times when I saw one hundred year old trees with huge roots, that were literally pulled out of the ground by the force of the water. That is a vivid picture of what will happen in your life when your gifts and talents break forth. They will remove and overcome every obstacle standing between you and your miracle. My friend, every breakthrough you need is located in your gift.

There is a close and direct connection between your gifts, your progress, and your favor. Most people have not made this connection, so their struggles continue. Your gifts and talents were given to you to help you prosper and succeed in life. Child of God, when your gift is working, favor and progress are released in order that your greatness and dominion may be established in the earth. Doors will be opened that no man can shut. This principle is powerfully demonstrated in the lives of two of my favorite Bible prophets, Joseph and Daniel. Both men arrived as slaves in the lands of their captivity. However, because of their commitment to God, He favored them and caused them to burst forth like the breaking forth of water. Because of God's favor, they eventually rose to occupy the most outstanding positions in their land. They had one gift in common, a God-given ability to interpret dreams. This divine gift brought them into prominence, and gave them powerful, influential roles in the palace of the king.

In Joseph's case, his gift took him from prison to the palace in one day. *"And Pharaoh said unto his servants, Can we find such a one as this is, a man in whom the Spirit of God is? And Pharaoh said unto Joseph, Forasmuch as God hath shewed thee all this, there is none so discreet and wise as thou art: Thou shalt be over my house, and according unto thy word shall all my people be ruled: only in the throne will I be greater than thou. And Pharaoh said unto Joseph, See, I have set thee over all the land of Egypt. And Pharaoh took off his ring from his hand, and put it upon Joseph's hand, and arrayed him in vestures of fine linen, and put a gold chain about his neck; And he made him to ride in the second chariot which he had; and they cried before him, Bow the knee: and he made him ruler over all the land of Egypt," (Genesis 41:38-43).*

I would say that Joseph's gift definitely made room for him! Even Pharaoh, with all his training in ancient wisdom, immediately conceded that someone greater than he had come. In one instant, every obstacle before Joseph came crumbling down. This was because his gift was bursting forth as he diligently, patiently interpreted the dreams of Pharaoh. One night, this brother went to bed a prisoner, but within twenty-four hours, he became the second greatest man in all of Egypt. That is what your gift can do. My question to you is, "Do you know your gift?"

When Your Gift Is Operating, God's Favor Is Released

Like Joseph, Daniel was also a slave in captivity. However, he had one thing which caused the favor of God to break forth in his life. This was his ability to interpret dreams, which was his gift. Daniel also feared and loved God, and this caused his life, even as Joseph's, to be garnished with favor. The Scripture tells us that, *"Daniel purposed in his heart that he would not defile himself with the portion of the king's meat, nor with the wine which he drank: therefore he requested of the prince of the eunuchs that he might not defile himself. Now God had brought Daniel into favor and tender love with the prince of the eunuchs," (Daniel 1:8-9).*

The Bible says that God will bless those who love righteousness. *"Thou hast loved righteousness, and hated iniquity; therefore God, even thy God, hath anointed thee with the oil of gladness above thy fellows," (Hebrews 1:9)*. This is what happened to Daniel.

Daniel was a man whose gift brought him into unusual promotion. Remember what I said earlier – your gift was given to you in order that you may be a blessing to someone else. Until your gift becomes a solution to someone's problem, there will be no reward. Child of God, if you honor the Lord with your life, He will create situations where your gifts and talents can be recognized and celebrated. Just like Pharaoh of Egypt, Nebuchadnezzar of Babylon had a disturbing dream which none of his magicians, astrologers or sorcerers could interpret. Moreover, the king demanded that his sorcerers recall his personal dream! The Scripture tells us that because the wise men were unable to tell, nor interpret the dream, they were all summoned to be killed.

"For this cause the king was angry and very furious, and commanded to destroy all the wise men of Babylon. And the decree went forth that the wise men should be slain; and they sought Daniel and his fellows to be slain. Then Daniel answered with counsel and wisdom to Arioch the captain of the king's guard, which was gone forth to slay the wise men of Babylon: He answered and said to Arioch the king's captain, Why is the decree so hasty from the king? Then Arioch made the thing known to Daniel," (Daniel 2:12-15).

This is so beautiful! Many times, God will create problems, just so His children can solve them. When we become problem-solvers, men will bless us!

"Then was the secret revealed unto Daniel in a night vision. Then Daniel blessed the God of Heaven." Daniel 2:19

"Therefore Daniel went in unto Arioch, whom the king had ordained to destroy the wise men of Babylon: he went and said thus unto him; Destroy not the wise men of Babylon: bring me in before the king, and I will show unto the king the interpretation." Daniel 2:24

After Daniel interpreted Nebuchadnezzar's dream, he was promoted to a position where he was second in command after the king.

"Then the king Nebuchadnezzar fell upon his face, and worshipped Daniel, and commanded that they should offer an oblation and sweet odors unto him. The king answered unto Daniel, and said, Of a truth it is, that your God is a God of gods, and a Lord of kings, and a revealer of secrets, seeing thou couldest reveal this secret. Then the king made Daniel a great man, and gave him many great gifts, and made him ruler over the whole province of Babylon, and chief of the governors over all the wise men of Babylon." Daniel 2:46-48

The favor of God is so powerful that it made a king bow down to his slave in worship. Nebuchadnezzar also made Daniel a great ruler over the entire land. Those who were with Daniel also came into great blessing. *"Then Daniel requested of the king, and he set Shadrach, Meshach, and Abednego, over the affairs of the province of Babylon: but Daniel sat in the gate of the king,"* (Daniel 2:49).

Locating Your Kingdom Gift

The success God has for you is linked to the gifts and talents He has already put inside you. As I mentioned before, your activated and developed gifts are a prelude to your destiny. All your talents are divine confirmation of God's plan to bless you and make you an enviable success. However this will not just happen automatically. You have to do something about it. Remember that, *"A man's gift maketh room for him and bringeth him before great men,"* *(Proverbs 18:16)*.

In order for you to rule in life during these challenging times, you must know your voice and your gift. Your gift was given to you by God for trading.

"He that tilleth his land shall have plenty of bread: but he that followeth after vain persons shall have poverty enough." *Proverbs 28:19*

Your land is your gift, and those who work it shall have plenty of bread.

Your Gift Is Your Sweet Spot

Have you found your sweet spot? Have you discovered that thing which brings you the most joy? Until you find that voice, your life is only an experiment. My friend, would you agree with me that God deserves more out of your life than what you are giving Him today? Jesus died so that you can be the best you. So let me ask you a question, "Are you the best you?" Only you can answer that question.

Thirteen years ago, I made the decision to be the best me possible. In doing so, I went on a long journey to decode all my gifts and talents. Today, I know what I am good at (and what I am not). My gift is very simple–I am a messenger. I have been divinely chosen by God to carry a message to my world. I enter the lives of people, not by chance, but by divine order and plan. My purpose is to connect them back to their Source. In order to accomplish my mission, I do six things:

* Pray   * Study
* Read   * Coach
* Write   * Teach

This is what I do, and it brings me the most joy. When I am doing these six things, I am in my element. I can even go for days without eating. "Why is this?" you may ask. Because when I am doing these activities, I flow with ease, and time disappears. I have found my sweet spot. This is what I am wired for. Anything outside of these six things is a complete distraction for me. May I be honest with you? When I find myself doing other things outside my calling, I encounter difficulties. I sweat a lot and become very anxious. I feel like a fish out of water.

In the early days, we did not have people to help us, so indeed I did do everything. But this was more out of necessity than desire. My hand was in everything. I was the bookkeeper, accountant, sound board man, and cleaner. I was the jack-of-all-trades, but I did quite a lousy job of them all. I even ran the camera to capture myself while preaching...(just joking)! Now, all those jobs are needed to keep a ministry moving forward, but I do not have to do it all. For example, I enjoy graphic design. I love the idea of putting thoughts on paper. Realistically, though, I do not have enough time to indulge in those activities. I need to focus on my calling, and doing those six things that God wired me to do.

Dear friend, please do yourself a favor and admit, as I did, that you are not Superman. You do not have to strive to do everything. Occupy your time doing what you love, and find people to staff your weaknesses. For example, administration is not my strongest gifting. As a matter-of-fact, I hate it, but without administrative work, nothing would move forward. So, I knew I needed to staff my weaknesses. As a result, I found people who are good at those things and enjoy them, like my wife. Bless her heart! Today, we have a great administrative staff, which is led by my wife. They make me look good, and they love what they do. Now you know why – because it is their gift.

Ten Keys to Recognize

Your Gifts, Talents and Purpose

The success God has for you is linked to your gifts, talents and Kingdom purpose. He has already put them inside you.

1. Your gift is your sweet spot–something you are very good at, and enjoy doing. Locate the thing which brings you the most joy, and spend your time doing that. If you want to be a success, do not allow yourself to be distracted by engaging in activities that keep you from your element.

2. What is the desire of your heart? Your joy and destiny are locked up in your heart. Your heart's desire can also be your destiny crying out.

3. What causes you the greatest pain? Whatever grieves you is a clue to something you are called to heal. My greatest pain is to see people suffering from sickness and lack. Every time I come in contact with those devils, I become angry. I hate sickness, and I despise poverty with a passion.

4. What stirs your passion? Your passion is the voice of destiny crying out for expression. Your passion is your zeal, fire and excitement. It is the intensity you feel on the inside toward something important to you.

5. What do mature people see in you? I believe in the prophetic ministry of our Lord Jesus. God has used many

mature brothers and sisters to speak the Word of the Lord into my life. Do not open yourself up to just anyone. Measure a person's life, not just his words. I have been blessed by my exposure to many choice servants of God who can hear from Heaven. When you recognize that a mature person of God has come into your presence, be watchful for what they have to say.

6. Where do you have fruit? Every tree is known by its fruit. The areas of your life where there are fruit and blessing are the areas of your gift and calling. Please do not waste time doing things you are not called to do! Where there is fruit, there is life, and where there is life, there is God. Locate the fruit in your life, and you will have clues to your calling.

7. Which thoughts, visions and dreams are impossible to leave your mind? Everything God does in your life begins with a thought or a vision. When the Lord told my wife and I to start a ministry in Canada, we could not get the idea out of our minds. Even though we did not have any money, we had faith, and faith gave our thoughts and vision substance.

8. What flows naturally out of you? I love to help and minister to people in need. This is the easiest thing for me to do. Four years ago, my wife and I were in Switzerland ministering at *Touch The Love Ministries* with our dear friends, Pastors Hartmut & Marietta Olschewsky. One night, I ministered until four in morning. The glory of God was so thick that no one wanted to leave the church. After ministering for eight hours, any natural person would have been very tired, but I was not. There was such a sweet flow of healing, blessing and prophecy. The more I ministered to the people, the fresher I became.

This book was actually birthed during that glory meeting. My point in telling this story is to encourage you to locate your natural flow and stay with it. Wherever your flow is: singing, writing, planning, teaching, administration or dancing – go for it!

9. Which areas of your life, ministry or career do you feel the peace of God about pursuing? Our wonderful God will use His peace to guide you into your future. When you are in your element and on course with God, you will have an abundance of peace. Remember, your element is what you were born to do. It is your gifts, talents, and purpose combined, and when you are flowing in your element, you will have great joy.

10. What is the witness of the Spirit? God has a million ways to let us know what is right, what is wrong, and what His will is. Some call the witness a feeling, a knowing, intuition, or a green light on the inside. We all have a witness in our Spirit when we need to make a decision. Pay very close attention to the witness in your Spirit, because that is God speaking.

CHAPTER SIXTEEN

THE POWER OF MENTORSHIP FOR SUCCESS

"That ye be not slothful, but followers of them who through faith and patience inherit the promises."
Hebrews 6:12

G od does not want us to struggle to achieve our dreams and goals! He desires to speed up the process of our breakthroughs by bringing us into relationship with life-tested mentors. Throughout history, great leaders who stood on the shoulders of mentors have risen to positions of influence. This has enabled them to achieve great things.

There are many examples of success mentoring in the Bible. We see how Joshua was able to develop his leadership skills through his covenant relationship with Moses. The prophet Elijah mentored Elisha in the ways of the Spirit. Jesus was the ultimate prototype of success, and He flawlessly modeled the ways of His Father before Peter and His other disciples. Do you ever wonder why the saints were so successful in accomplishing their Kingdom assignments? The answer lies in their mentorship.

Our opening Scripture tells us to be followers of them who through faith and patience inherit the promises. This is a success principle which produces results in the lives of those who will work it. When Dr. Martin Luther King Jr. needed fresh inspiration with which to fight racial segregation in the United States, he turned to the teachings of Mahatma Gandhi. Luther's nonviolent approach to leadership that he learned from Gandhi became the catalyst that melted hearts. Today we still talk about his exploits! As we look through the pages of history, we will observe the principle of mentorship at work over and over again. Those who respect mentorship reap great rewards.

Who Is a Mentor?

A mentor is a wise and trusted counselor or teacher who desires to add value to his or her protégé. He assists his protégé to locate and develop personal gifts and skills. A mentor will also shorten the seasons of hardship in the life of his protégé. He helps his student to see the big picture, and how to define and achieve personal success within that picture. I think one of the greatest gifts we can obtain in life is to have someone guide and lead us into what we desire to become. John Maxwell, renowned leadership speaker, once said, "You will never knew how much you are missing until you are willing to open your heart to a trusted mentor."

Follow After Success

Success is neither a miracle, nor a matter of luck. On the contrary, success is habitually practicing laws until the desired results manifest. I like something that Brian Tracy, motivational speaker and author, once said, "If you are absolutely clear about what you want in life, you can probably achieve it by studying the lives of those who have achieved the same goal. And by doing what they did, you can get the same results."

Wow, this is powerful! If you want to succeed, follow successful people. My friend, God in His mercy has placed people in our pathways who are equipped to bring out the best in us. No man is an island unto himself; we need each other. The Bible says, *"Thus saith the Lord, Stand ye in the ways, and see, and ask for the old paths, where is the good way, and walk therein, and ye shall find rest for your souls. But they said, We will not walk therein," (Jeremiah 6:16).*

Show me a man who has no mentor and I will show you a man whose life is full of struggles, woes and sadness. Every great leader is an offspring of another. If you do not have any mentor you are following, there may never be another who follows you. In the book of Hebrews we are admonished to, *"... be not slothful, but followers of them who through faith and patience inherit the promises," (Hebrews 6:12).*

This Scripture is very clear regarding mentorship. Over and over, I have heard proud people say, "I follow Jesus, but I will not follow men." You have likely heard this as well. This statement sounds good, but it is rooted in pride and unbelief. My friend, if this is your thinking, you are fighting against the Word of God, and you cannot win. There is great merit in humbling yourself to sit at the feet of a mentor. You will learn things while simply serving in the ministry of your mentor that would take you years to learn otherwise, if you would learn them at all.

Hear words that came straight from the lips of our Master, *"And if ye have not been faithful in that which is another man's, who shall give you that which is your own?" (Luke 16:12).* These are not the words of man, but of Jesus Himself, and are therefore the highest form of wisdom.

In 1997, I had just finished Bible school when a prophet named Jim Maloney came to my city. He pointed his finger in my direction and called me out from an audience of about three hundred spiritually hungry people. He spoke words over me that changed my life forever. This is what he declared:

"The Lord thy God has released unto you this day an Elijah. When you see him, you will know him, and when you meet him, follow him because I have ordained him to raise you up."

Three day later, I met Apostle Charles Ndifon. He took my wife and I under his wings. When many did not believe in us, he did. A few months after meeting him, my wife and I sold all our earthly possessions and moved our little family to the United States, to be mentored by Apostle Charles and his wife. We have traveled to countless nations of the world together, preaching the power of the Gospel. We have seen thousands healed, saved and set free. Even more than that, we have seen thousands come into a new sense of purpose in Christ. My man of God has taken me places in the Spirit that words cannot describe.

I remember one sunny afternoon, we were in the nation of Zimbabwe, and we went into a little hospice hospital. That is right, it was a hospice hospital. During the next thirty minutes, as we walked through the rooms, eight people were discharged from the gates of death. I thank God every day for my man of God. Let me repeat again what John Maxwell said, "You will never know how much you are missing, until you are willing to open your heart to a trusted mentor."

Mentorship Brings Exposure

Exposure comes by association. Your associations determine your level of exposure in life, business or ministry. You have to make a decision to learn from those who are operating at the level you want to go. Expose your mind to that level by reading their books, and by humbling your heart to serve when an opportunity presents itself. Do everything possible to be in their presence. Every year I always seek an opportunity to have my mentors lay their hands on me. I am convinced that this is one of the secrets for fresh oil on my life: *"Let thy garments be always white; and let thy head lack no ointment,"* *(Ecclesiastes 9:8).*

When a person is exposed to something greater than they have known, they will not go back. You can influence someone's life by exposing them to something better and greater. Exposure affects desires.

Exposure Breeds Greatness

I believe the reason why Joshua was so bold and successful is that he was directly connected to Moses, his mentor and father in the spirit. Joshua served Moses.

"The Lord said to Moses, Take Joshua son of Nun, a man in whom is the Spirit, and lay your hand upon him; And set him before Eleazar the priest and all the congregation and give him a charge in their sight. And put some of your honor and authority upon him, that all the congregation of the Israelites may obey him....And Moses did as the Lord commanded him. He took Joshua and set him before Eleazar the priest and all the congregation." Numbers 27:18-20, 22 (AMP)

Let me ask you some questions. Who is your father? Who is your Moses? Who is your pastor? Who is the one that is pouring oil on your head? Please find your Moses! This generation is too prideful to sit and serve. They do not want to wait until their appointed time has come. Everybody wants something without paying for it. They want resurrection, without the crucifixion. I am so glad that this was not the mindset of Joshua, and I am even more glad it was not the mindset of Jesus.

The Lord told me years ago that if I desired to be a successful minister in Canada, I needed to expose my mind to men and women of God who have gone before me, and tap into what they are doing. For example, every time I listen to Bishop David Oyedepo, or read his books, something always happens to me on the inside. His books are full of fire! His faith and his words are always a source of inspiration to me. I cannot listen to him without dreaming bigger. He stretches my imagination to do something big for the Kingdom. He is one of those ministers who challenges me to go beyond myself, and to be ready to pay the price in order for my generation to be saved. That price may come in different forms, but by the grace of God, I am willing to pay it like Bishop David Oyedepo did.

My friend, we all need this type of influence in our lives, to challenge and motivate us to the higher life. If you lack mentorship in your life, you are limiting your potential. Check your circle of friends, and ask yourself some deep questions. A good one to start with is, "Who are the biggest influences in my life?"

At Harvard University, a study was done on the law of influence. This study concluded that there are only three groups of people in the world. These are:

A. Those who add value to our lives.
B. Those who multiply our effectiveness.
C. Those who take from us and add nothing.

When I look at that list, I am no longer uncertain of who will be in my life. Choosing the right people can either make you or break you, because associations determine your level of exposure and reward.

When you have a vision or dream to accomplish great things with God, you must be certain to have His input in deciding your friendships and associations. You cannot just marry anyone! Who you marry can either make you or break you. I have seen many life destinies end in frustration and unfruitfulness because of wrong choices in marriage. My wife and I have been married now for almost twenty years. To this day, we have never had a fight over the call of God. So know what you want in life, and with God's help, He will bring you into the right relationships. This is so important, because your associations determine your level of exposure, which in turn affects your perceptions.

The caliber of people you associate with can determine the level of your reward. I have disciplined myself to read two to three books a month to keep myself abreast of the knowledge necessary to fulfill my mission. Some of the books I read are written by people who are still alive, while others are written by people who have gone home to be with the Lord. Where they are is not important. What matters is that when I read their books, I am associating with them and exposing myself to their thoughts, spirits, and successes.

Why We Study and Follow Successful People

I have studied the lives of successful people and try to do what they are doing. I am not ashamed to say that. Life is too short for me to waste time reinventing the wheel. I like something that Brian Tracy says, "When you desire something great, find someone who has done it and do the same thing."

I have many mentors who I follow diligently. Some are Christians and some are not. For personal development and excellence in life management, I humbly sit at the feet of Brian Tracy, Tony Robbins, and Myles Munroe. For spiritual dominion and apostolic authority in my set place as a man of God, I gladly lean on the chest of Bishop David Oyedepo. For the sweet anointing that causes things to happen in my life without struggle I glean from the ministry of Pastor Chris Oyakhilome. For financial dominion I learn from Kenneth Copeland, Bill Winston and Mike Murdock. For lessons in success for marriage and family there is no one like Silas and Jennifer Johnson. Last but not least, my pastor and spiritual father Apostle Charles Ndifon, who embodies the Spirit of love, has taught me how to live from the heart of God. These are my mentors, and they have made my life very rich in God.

Ten Benefits of Having a Mentor

1. They shorten your season of frustration.

2. They cause influential people to listen to you by transferring credibility.

3. They bring you into great exposure by their associations with you.

4. They become enemies to your enemy by paralyzing the work of satan.

5. They put fear in the heart of satan when they call your name in prayer.

6. They transfer wisdom to their protégés.

7. They help establish the financial thermostat in the life of their protégés.

8. They can transfer prophetic insight to their protégés.

9. They can bring you into uncommon favor and prophetic experience.

10. They can help their protégés to discover their calling in Christ.

I may not be the most talented individual, but when it comes to knowledge and success, I might be the hungriest person you will ever meet. I credit this to my mentors.

CHAPTER SEVENTEEN

THE PSYCHOLOGY OF WEALTH

"Every place that the sole of your foot shall tread upon, that have I given unto you, as I said unto Moses." Joshua 1:3

"And He brought him forth abroad, and said, Look now toward Heaven, and tell the stars, if thou be able to number them: and He said unto him, So shall thy seed be." Genesis 15:5

What you see is what you get.

If you cannot see it, you will not taste it!

I called this chapter, *The Psychology Of Wealth*, because most people have deeply rooted problems in their thinking regarding wealth. To set them free, a radical shift in their mind and spirit is necessary. Your mind is where everything begins for you! You have to take extreme mental action in order to have breakthrough in the mind. Until you change your thoughts, you cannot change your life. If you want to change your outer world of poverty, you must first purge your inside thought world of lack and shortages.

I have studied the power of self-image for the last thirteen years. Because of my past, this has become one of my favorite subjects. I have come to the conclusion that there is a deep connection between your net worth and your self-worth. How you see yourself affects your money. You may not believe this, but it is true! The day my wife and I started improving our self-images was the catalyst for everything to begin changing in our lives. Our friends, finances and influence all changed. I have proven this principle in many nations of the world. People are people, whether they are black, white, yellow or brown. If your self-image is low, your flow of money will be low as well. No one can stop you from succeeding, but yourself!

If you have a healthy self-image, the force of the Kingdom within you will magnetically attract all the finances you need to fulfill your destiny. When your self-image is good, so will be your supply of money. This is a law which cannot be changed by anyone.

> **"When your self-worth goes up,**
> **Your net worth goes up with it."**
> **- Mark Victor Hansen**

Child of God, your Father desires to do some great things in your life, and I believe this is one of the reasons this book has come into your hands. He has chosen you to manifest His dreams and aspirations, and as you read and accept these divine secrets, His dream will begin to grow in you.

I can see God's dream of victory, success, hope, love, intelligence and possibilities breaking forth into your life!

Nothing happens by chance. You have been chosen out of many millions to come in contact with these truths, and as you renew your mind to them, you will be catapulted into a life of greatness. Even more importantly, you will break free from the prison of your past.

In my past, I missed out on so much because of low self-esteem, but no more! I still remember those dark, cold nights like it was yesterday; no one desired me. No one cared. I was just a shadow in the dark. But then something happened. Jesus came! The first thing I saw in Jesus was confidence. His self-image was impeccable. There was no poor self-image in the Son of God. He was humble, yet self-assured. He knew Who He was. He knew His origin was in God. Listen to what He says, *"He that cometh from above is above all: he that is of the earth is earthly, and speaketh of the earth: He that cometh from Heaven is above all," (John 3:31).* Then, with great boldness, He declares, *"Ye are from beneath; I am from above: ye are of this world; I am not of this world." John 8:23*

Now these statements are too much for the religious mind! Jesus would have been cast out of most churches in the western world for uttering them.

"For the Father loveth the Son, and sheweth Him all things that Himself doeth: and He will shew Him greater works than these, that ye may marvel." John 5:20

Glory to God, I feel like singing!

"Jesus said unto them, Verily, verily, I say unto you, Before Abraham was, I AM." John 8:58

Does this sound like a weak man? Does this sound like a man who was so possessed by the spirit of poverty that He had no place to lay His head? My friend, this poverty thinking is demonic and deceives people into believing that the perfect Son of God was poor. This is insulting and shameful, and a direct attack against the nature of God. Jesus promises that those connected to Him will have an abundant life, filled with provision, love, joy, peace and the pleasure of His fellowship – a glorious, brilliant, overcoming life!

"Then spake Jesus again unto them, saying, I am the light of the world: he that followeth me shall not walk in darkness, but shall have the light of life," (John 8:12).

The Poor Have No Voice

The very fact that multitudes of people were following Jesus is one of the proofs that He was not poor, because a poor man's wisdom is despised, and his words are not heard.

"Wisdom is better than strength: nevertheless the poor man's wisdom is despised, and his words are not heard," (Ecclesiastes 9:16).

I would be interested to see a poor man attempting to lead the world and expecting to have people following him. That would be a sight to behold.

The church today cannot handle Jesus. If He were here in the flesh today, preaching in church, He would be accused of thinking too much of Himself. To have His kind of confidence seems too outrageous for some; however His confidence was the reason for His success. He knew no fear, mocked poverty, and confronted kings. He overcame the world and triumphed over death. I love Him. He is my hero, my friend and my self-image. I gave up all my fears and inadequacies and received His fullness instead. I gave up my poor self-image, and when I did, everything changed. Now I stand complete in His perfection. When I fall short, which happens many times, I am strengthened by His love for me! I see good things ahead for you my friend, but you have to stop the thief – the devil.

The Good Life Is Yours

"The thief comes only in order to steal and kill and destroy. I came that they may have and enjoy life, and have it in abundance (to the full, till it overflows)." John 10:10 (AMP)

I love this life our Master brought us, yet so many of God's children are not enjoying this good life. Why? They refuse to change their thinking. Yes, they love the Lord, but being a Christian does not guarantee success. This is very sad, but many who are bound for Heaven are earthly failures. They refuse to change their picture of themselves. Child of God, your internal vision determines the boundaries of your blessing. What you see is what you really get. When you change the way you think financially, it will change your financial world.

Your Imagination Is a Preview of What Is Possible

How you see yourself in your imagination determines everything else about you. Your mindset determines your assets. Now, at this moment I would like to reprogram you with more thoughts concerning success and money. If you accept these seeds and follow the leading of the Holy Spirit, things will start looking greater and better for you. I will share with you reasons why it was impossible for Jesus to be poor. Is that a new thought for you? Well, fasten your seat belt!

The Wealth of Jesus

Child of God, the Spirit of greatness is working in you. By virtue of redemption, everything Jesus is, so are you in this world. One of the many graces, or offices, Jesus walked in was the office of Kingship. Jesus was not only a Prophet, He was also a King, and every king is business minded. Even from His youth, Jesus was very conscious of doing His Father's business.

Heirs of All Things

A king's domain is manifested in his wealth. Jesus was the most wealthy King, and He brought every grace to this earth. He said that His Kingdom was not of this world. In Luke's Gospel, Jesus strengthens this thought even more.

"And I appoint unto you a Kingdom, as My Father hath appointed unto Me; That ye may eat and drink at My table in My kingdom, and sit on thrones judging the twelve tribes of Israel." Luke 22:29-30

A king is a rightful owner of lands, livestock and material substances like gold, silver, oil and other resources. The Bible speaks about the seven-fold blessing of Jesus.

"Saying with a loud voice, Worthy is the Lamb that was slain to receive power, and riches, and wisdom, and strength, and honor, and glory, and blessing." Revelation 5:12

All these things were part of Jesus' inheritance after He defeated the little devil. God has appointed His Son to be heir of all things.

"Hath in these last days spoken unto us by His Son, whom He hath appointed Heir of all things, by Whom also He made the worlds." Hebrews 1:2

This is beautiful! Jesus was appointed as Heir and Ruler of all things. Do you see it? JESUS IS HEIR of ALL THINGS, and He gladly shares them with us. Glory be to God!

How Wealthy Was Jesus?

Dead religion has told us that Jesus was very poor. Let us be honest with ourselves, do you really believe the Son of God was poor? Be careful with your answer, because your answer could reveal many things about your faith!

Let us find out whether Jesus was poor. First of all, in the mind of a Jew, to be poor is to be worse than an infidel (someone without a covenant with God), *(1 Timothy 5:8, KJV)*. Poverty was even considered a curse, according to the Word of God, *(Deuteronomy 28:15-40)*. Even more so, for a rabbi (teacher) to be poor and cursed was unheard of. In order to qualify as a rabbi, a man had to be upright in all aspects of the law. He was also required to be an example to all the people he was leading. Because poverty was regarded as a curse resulting from sin, no security guard would have given Jesus privileged access to the temple, if He were poverty stricken. The Bible says that Jesus customarily went into the synagogue to preach, *(Matthew 4:23-24)*. The synagogue was the most holy place of that day, and strictly off limits to sinners; which Jesus would be if He was poor, according to the law.

To be poverty stricken means exactly what it says: to be struck with a curse that keeps you in a continual state of lack. And material curses can only come through the sin of disobedience, according to the law.

"And thou shalt not go aside from any of the words which I command thee this day, to the right hand, or to the left, to go after other gods to serve them. But it shall come to pass, if thou wilt not hearken unto the voice of the Lord thy God, to observe to do all His commandments and His statutes which I command thee this day; that all these curses shall come upon thee, and overtake thee." Deuteronomy 28:14-15

These are the curses God speaks of in *Deuteronomy Chapter 28:16-48*. They come to those who break the law because of their disobedience.

Ten Curses of Disobedience

"Cursed shall thou be in the city, and cursed shall thou be in the field." (v 16)

"Cursed shall be thy basket and thy store." (v 17)

"Cursed shall be the fruit of thy body, and the fruit of thy land, the increase of thy kine, and the flocks of thy sheep." (v 18)

"Cursed shall thou be when thou comest in, and cursed shall thou be when thou goest out." (v 19)

"The Lord shall send upon thee cursing, vexation, and rebuke, in all that thou settest thine hand unto to do, until thou be destroyed, and until thou perish quickly; because of the wickedness of thy doings, whereby thou hast forsaken Me." (v 20)

"The Lord shall smite thee with madness, and blindness, and astonishment of heart." (v 28)

"And thou shall grope at noonday, as the blind gropeth in darkness, and thou shall not prosper in thy ways: and thou shall be only oppressed and spoiled evermore, and no man shall save thee." (v 29)

"Thine ox shall be slain before thine eyes, and thou shall not eat thereof: thine ass shall be violently taken away from before thy face, and shall not be restored to thee: thy sheep shall be given unto thine enemies, and thou shall have none to rescue them." (v 31)

"Thou shall carry much seed out into the field, and shall gather but little in; for the locust shall consume it." (v 38)

"Therefore shall thou serve thine enemies which the Lord shall send against thee, in hunger, and in thirst, and in nakedness, and in want of all things: and he shall put a yoke of iron upon thy neck, until he has destroyed thee." (v 48)

Now look at that list of curses. We can see there is a big problem if someone thinks Jesus was poor! First, if Jesus was disobedient to the voice of His Father, that alone would have disqualified Him from being the Savior of the world. Second, His entire claim to have power over sin, the world, and satan would be false. Third, His death, burial, and resurrection would be bogus. If that is true, then what we have been preaching for the last 2000 years is just a lie, and there is no Heaven or hell. This would also mean that the Bible is not true, and every preacher is a fake.

Well, they are wrong! My friend, it is spiritual suicide to go down that slippery road and question the authenticity of the Son of God. The alternative is to believe what the Bible says concerning God's righteous Servant, Whose joy was to always please His Father. Child of God, if there was anyone who was qualified to walk in all the promises of blessing as listed in

Deuteronomy 28:1-14, it was Jesus. He was the perfect Son of God, Who only did and said what He saw His Father do.

"Then Jesus answered and said to them, "Most assuredly, I say to you, the Son can do nothing of Himself, but what He sees the Father do; for whatever He does, the Son also does in like manner." John 5:19 (NKJV)

Let us look at some more thoughts to further illustrate the wealth of Jesus. Listen to what the Bible says about Abraham:

"And the Lord hath blessed my master greatly; and he is become great: and He hath given him flocks, and herds, and silver, and gold, and menservants, and maidservants, and camels, and asses." Genesis 24:35

Did you see that? *"And the Lord hath blessed my master greatly and he is become great!"*

Why in the world would God make other people very great with silver and gold, but fail to provide for His own Son? If that were true, it would be spiritual insanity and absolute hypocrisy. God would have had to break His own Word to do such a thing.

"But if any provide not for his own, and specially for those of his own house, he hath denied the faith, and is worse than an infidel." 1 Timothy 5:8

Eleven Biblical Reasons Why it was Impossible for Jesus To Be Poor

1. Jesus was the perfect Son of God (*John 1:1&14; Hebrews 7:28*).

2. Being poor would have been a sign that the curse was at work in Him, and it was impossible for the Son of God to be cursed (*Matthew 17:5*).

3. Poverty can only come through disobedience and sin, and the Son of God was always perfect in all His ways (*John 6:38*).

4. Jesus was too anointed for the curse of satan to work in His life (*Luke 4:18; Matthew 8:16*).

5. The blessing of *Deuteronomy 28:1-13* was resting on Jesus in fullness. He was an obedient Son, therefore the curse stayed away (*Luke 2:51-52; Matthew 26:42*).

6. Jesus was the source of wisdom, therefore wealth was always at His command *(John 1:2-3; Matthew 17:27)*.

7. The curse of poverty had no access to Jesus' life, because He was sinless, and knew no sin (*2 Corinthians 5:21*).

8. Jesus was anointed by the Holy Spirit to bring deliverance to those who were afflicted by shortages and famine. In the spirit, you can only give what you already have (*Matthew 14:19*).

9. Jesus was a King and it is impossible for a king to be poor, because his dominion is manifested by his wealth (*John 3:35; John 16:15*).

10. Jesus was a Creator, so He could create whatever was lacking in His life (*Matthew 3:9; Hebrews 1:2*).

11. Jesus was and is the Ruler and Heir of all things. (*John 16:15; Revelation 5:12*).

Ten Facts Verifying the Wealth of King Jesus

1. Wealthy wise men came to see Him (*Matthew 2:1-2*).

2. Gold was given to Him at His birth (*Matthew 2:11*).

3. He had twelve inner circle staff, and another seventy working with Him (*Matthew 10:1-4; Luke 10:1*).

4. He traveled in ships, large and small (*Mark 4:36*).

5. His ministry was partnered by the rich and famous of His day (*Luke 8:1-3*).

6. He wore very expensive clothes (*John 19:23-24*).

7. He was born rich, but He became poor (*2 Corinthians 8:9*).

8. Every beast of the forest, and the cattle on a thousand hills belong to Him (*Psalm 50:10*).

9. He knows every fowl of the mountains (*Psalm 50:11*).

10. The entire world and all its fullness belong to Him (*Psalm 50:12b*).

My friend, you can look at that list and see for yourself that it would have been impossible for Jesus to be poor, and to be the Son of God. Jesus was very business minded. He was also a King, and every king in the Bible was wealthy!

CHAPTER EIGHTEEN

WINNING OVER LACK AND POVERTY

"Christ hath redeemed us from the curse of the law, being made a curse for us: for it is written, Cursed is every one that hangeth on a tree: That the blessing of Abraham might come on the Gentiles through Jesus Christ; that we might receive the promise of the Spirit through faith."
Galatians 3:13-14

Lack is not a game, it is a curse. I hate it with a passion. Lack destroys the dreams and hopes of many families. As a child, I saw firsthand how this spirit almost destroyed my family.

When I was fifteen, my mother died from a disease which could have been prevented with proper food and good nutrition. These were things we could not afford for her because we were broke. I saw my father struggle with a basic eye problem that could have been solved with just simple drops, but he was deprived this comfort because we did not have money to buy them. This simply remedied problem eventually resulted in him becoming partially blind. Many years later, he died before his time due to a lack of good nutrition.

So you see, my issue with lack and poverty is very personal. I vow to expose this stinking poverty spirit and rid the earth of it. How? By teaching biblical solutions that will help people eradicate poverty and lack from their lives.

There Is Always a Cause

"As the bird by wandering, as the swallow by flying,
so the curse causeless shall not come." Proverbs 26:2

For every curse that anyone experiences, there must be a cause. In order for lack and poverty to function in the earth, there must be a cause. If we can cure the root cause, the fruit will be healed. That is my intention in this book – to bring healing to the root. Poverty should not exist on earth, because there is enough wealth for every human being to live a life of comfort and blessing. Just like there is abundance of oxygen, there is also abundance of wealth. Poverty and lack are rooted in a curse. They are not normal. As I said earlier, every curse must have a reason to function. Remove the cause and the problem will cease to exist.

Eight Reasons Why There Is so Much Poverty

1. Ignorance of Redemptive Truth

This is one of the biggest reasons why there is so much lack and shortage in the lives of people. There is no shortage in the earth, but there is lack in the lives of people. Nevertheless, the earth is full of riches. How can this happen? Because of lack of knowledge.

"My people are destroyed for lack of knowledge: because thou hast rejected knowledge, I will also reject thee, that thou shalt be no priest to Me: seeing thou hast forgotten the law of thy God, I will also forget thy children." Hosea 4:6

"Therefore My people are gone into captivity, because they have no knowledge: and their honorable men are famished, and their multitude dried up with thirst." Isaiah 5:13

The world has rejected the Lord, but they have accepted His principles for success. The church has accepted Jesus, but rejected His principles. Many have no knowledge of who they really are and this has caused problems. Just as knowledge is power, ignorance is deadly.

2. Ignorance of Identity

Many people are poor because they have no knowledge of who they are. They have failed to recognize their uniqueness, so they struggle unnecessarily. Do you know who you are? Until you do, you will not know what you are capable of. Your greatness is locked up in knowing who you are. So who are you?

"Behold, what manner of love the Father hath bestowed upon us, that we should be called the sons of God: therefore the world knoweth us not, because it knew Him not. Beloved, now are we the sons of God, and it doth not yet appear what we shall be: but we know that, when He shall appear, we shall be like Him; for we shall see Him as He is." 1 John 3:1-2

This is a powerful revelation! If you accept that you are truly God's son, and act in accordance with that position, you will bind the spirit of poverty and enjoy the freedom of your kingly son-ship. To be the son of a king is to be an heir to the kingdom. What does it mean to be an heir of God, you might ask? Well, it means that whatever belongs to God belongs to you! We are not only God's heirs, but joint heirs with Christ.

"The Spirit itself beareth witness with our spirit, that we are the children of God: And if children, then heirs; heirs of God, and

joint heirs with Christ; if so be that we suffer with Him, that we may be also glorified together." Romans 8:16-17

Webster defines an *heir* as: one who receives, or is entitled to receive, any properties, possessions, endowments, or qualities from a parent or predecessors; also, the heir is the rightful future recipient or possessor of the kingdom.

The question is this, "If we are heirs of God, what possessions or qualities have we inherited from Him?" The answer is overwhelming simple and simply overwhelming! It seems quite certain the we have inherited all that God is, and all that God has. We have inherited all that He ever will be, and all that He will ever yet create or develop through the expansion and propagation of creation itself.

Seven Inheritances We Have Received From Our Father

1. Heirs of the world, because we are the true seed of Abraham (Romans 4:13).

2. Heirs according to the hope of eternal life (Titus 3:7).

3. Heirs of salvation (Hebrews 1:14).

4. Heirs of promise (Hebrews 6:17).

5. Heirs of righteousness (Hebrews 11:7).

6. Heirs of the grace of life (1 Peter 3:7).

7. Heirs of the Kingdom of God (James 2:5).

3. Ignorance of What We Possess

Three examples from the Bible that illustrate this are:

- Moses and his rod (Exodus, chapters 3:1-4:21).
- The widow and her pot of oil (2 Kings, chapter 4:1-37).
- Adam and his divine connection (Genesis, chapters 1:26-3:24).

Moses was unaware of the power of his rod. God had to show him. In your case, your rod could be the gifts or talents God has given you. Many times people are unaware of what they have because of childhood pain. Amazingly, thoughts and words spoken over a child can become their present mindset. Words such as: "You will never amount to anything!" "That is not possible for you" or "You are not smart enough," once planted in the mind of a child, begin to shape his view of life. When he accepts those lies and thoughts, they become strongholds in his thinking that hinder him in life.

You have gifts and talents, and they reveal a lot about who you are. The widow woman in 2 Kings, chapter 4 thought she had nothing but a little bit of oil, but what she had was enough to cancel her debt. God wants to reveal to us the talents He has given us. Many people go through life suffering and disappointed because they have accepted a lie and disregarded the gifts and talents God has given them.

4. Ignorance of What We Can Do

This was Peter's problem (see Matthew 14:28-31). He was walking on water, but then he let the wind and waves convince him that walking on water was impossible. He should have let them know that he was already walking on water, so it was too late to try and tell him that it was impossible! Similarly, do not let others convince you that you cannot do something, especially when it is something you have already been doing.

You absolutely must change your mindset about what you can do. Consider your gifts and talents and ask yourself, "What can I do now?" Don't wait for perfection! Put things in motion today. Find out what you can do and then go out and do it. You cannot be lazy and think things will just happen. Be accountable with your time. A successful person does not think of only working from nine until five. He is passionate and willing to go the extra mile to unlock his destiny.

There is an amazing story in the Bible that exemplifies this trait. In Genesis, Rebekah went the extra mile. I often call it the *Extra Mile University*. As a result, this caused Abraham's servant to notice her. He too understood the value of going the extra mile. So when she drew water, not only for the servant but also for all of his camels, he knew she was the right woman for Isaac (See *Genesis 24:15-26*).

5. Laziness Causes Failure

"Laziness is a secret ingredient that goes into failure.
But it's only kept a secret from the person who fails."
Robert Half

There is no future in life for a lazy person. Hard work is not an inviting word for many today. Some would rather watch five hours of television, talk on the phone all day, and keep doing things to sabotage their financial destiny. Others blame satan for their financial depletion. Here is what King Solomon says about such a lack of wisdom:

Laziness brings shame.
"He becometh poor that dealeth with a slack hand: but the hand of the diligent maketh rich. He that gathereth in summer is a wise son: but he that sleepeth in harvest is a son that causeth shame..." Proverbs 10:4-5

A slack hand leads to poverty.
"He becometh poor that dealeth with a slack hand: but the hand of the diligent maketh rich." Proverbs 10:4

Lazy people end up in forced labour without results.
"The hand of the diligent shall bear rule: but the slothful shall be under tribute." Proverbs 12:24

Lazy people are full of excuses.
"The sluggard will not plow by reason of the cold; therefore shall he beg in harvest, and have nothing." Proverbs 20:4

6. Procrastination Brings Poverty

Procrastination is the habit of putting off or delaying something that requires immediate attention. The question we need to ask ourselves is, why would someone delay something that needs immediate attention? I believe this would be due to some deeply rooted issue, such as fear, inadequate skills, or laziness.

Procrastination is a thief of time, money, and relationships. You have to be merciless with procrastination. In order to accomplish all God has called you to do, you must begin to apply yourself to actions. Action is food for champions! Every exploit in life comes with a price tag. People who characteristically apply actions separate themselves as being successful, from those who barely survive.

When we look in the Bible, we see how God created the world through His actions. He did not just wish the light would appear, or for the firmament to show up by itself. He did not wait to wonder what decision He needed to make. God knew something very crucial: things do not just happen, if you do not make them happen.

We also, must be convinced of what we are going to do. I will paraphrase one of Sir Isaac Newton's *laws of motion*: "Things tend to stay at rest until relevant forces are applied." The same principle is true in the spirit. Your greatness, blessing, breakthrough and prosperity tend to stay at rest until you make a conscious choice to move them in your direction. Wishful thinking is not a strategy. You have to keep moving.

7. Unfaithfulness Causes Poverty

Have you realized how difficult it is to find faithful people? Even King Solomon had that problem with people. *"Most men will proclaim everyone his own goodness: but a faithful man who can find?" Proverbs 20:6*

Pastor Tracy and I have made a covenant in our hearts to possess this secret virtue, because we refuse to be poor! After serving and working with the great man of God, Apostle Charles Ndifon, our hearts still jump for joy at the opportunity to carry his bags and put his Bible on the pulpit. And yes, we have been doing this for fifteen years with joy.

Many people seem to have a covenant with poverty because they fail to possess this secret virtue of faithfulness. My friend, every time God sends you an opportunity to serve, please do not run from it. This is because locked up in serving is secret wisdom that pushes back poverty and shortage from your life. I have seen many people start out serving the Lord with joy, but then their hearts become cold. When that happens, the things that were working for them before, stop working. Still, they do not make the connection. Let me ask you, "Are you faithful? Are you dependable?" I could tell you many sad stories of people I know whose situations would have been better, if only they had been faithful in the opportunities they had.

Deadly Sting of Unfaithfulness

Unfaithfulness leads to destruction.
"The integrity of the upright will guide them, but the perversity of the unfaithful will destroy them." Proverbs 11:3 (NKJV)

Unfaithful people are wicked and can do things to hurt you.
"A man shall eat well by the fruit of his mouth, but the soul of the unfaithful feeds on violence." Proverbs 13:2 (NKJV)

Unfaithfulness will always bring people hardships.
"Good understanding gains favor, but the way of the unfaithful is hard." Proverbs 13:15 (NKJV)

Unfaithfulness is a seed that instigates lust.
"The righteousness of the upright will deliver them, but the unfaithful will be caught by their lust." Proverbs 11:6 (NKJV)

Unfaithful people are very scary.
"Confidence in an unfaithful man in time of trouble is like a bad tooth and a foot out of joint." Proverbs 25:19 (NKJV)

8. Pride Also Brings Poverty

This is one of the biggest downfalls in the lives of many of God's people. Many have gone jobless because of pride. I have learned something from Dr. T.L. Osborn. He said, "Learn to sit on the floor until you can afford a stool. Sit on the stool until you can get a chair, and whatever you do, stay out of debt." Pride is the reason for poverty in the lives of many.

The Poison of Pride

Proud people end up in shame.
"When pride cometh, then cometh shame: but with the lowly is wisdom." Proverbs 11:2

God cannot stand the proud in heart. He closes the door of divine blessing on them.
"Whoso privily slandereth his neighbour, him will I cut off: him that hath an high look and a proud heart will not I suffer." Psalm 101:5

Pride will bring a man low, and that is what leads him to poverty.
"A man's pride shall bring him low: but honour shall uphold the humble in spirit." Proverbs 29:23

God will fight against the proud in heart.
"...Wherefore he saith, God resisteth the proud, but giveth grace unto the humble." James 4:6

Pride produces nothing good in the lives of those who allow it in them.
"Only by pride cometh contention: but with the well advised is wisdom." Proverbs 13:10

9. Disobedience Leads To Poverty

"If ye be willing and obedient, ye shall eat the good of the land." Isaiah 1:19

"All the commandments which I command thee this day shall ye observe to do, that ye may live, and multiply, and go in and possess the land which the Lord sware unto your fathers. And thou shalt remember all the way which the Lord thy God led thee these forty years in the wilderness, to humble thee, and to prove thee, to know what was in thine heart, whether thou wouldest keep His commandments, or no." Deuteronomy 8:1-2

10. Poverty Is Caused by a Curse

"But it shall come to pass, if thou wilt not harken unto the voice of the Lord thy God, to observe to do all His commandments and His statutes which I command thee this day; that all these curses shall come upon thee, and overtake thee: Cursed shalt thou be in the city, and cursed shalt thou be in the field. Cursed shall be thy basket and thy store. Cursed shall be the fruit of thy body, and the fruit of thy land, the increase of thy kine, and the flocks of thy sheep. Cursed shalt thou be when thou comest in, and cursed shalt thou be when thou goest out. The Lord shall send upon thee cursing, vexation, and rebuke, in all that thou settest thine hand unto for to do, until thou be destroyed, and until thou perish quickly; because of the wickedness of thy doings, whereby thou hast forsaken Me." Deuteronomy 28:15-20

CHAPTER NINETEEN

THE POWER OF ACTION

We will talk here about supernatural actions. Have you ever received a prophecy before? If you have, there will be some action required on your part to make the prophetic Word come to pass. Prophecies are messages from God–that's when you receive a prophetic Word or read the Bible and that Word pierces your heart and really excites you. That is the Holy Ghost speaking directly to you. I have more faith in the Word of God speaking to me than a prophet because a human agent can make a mistake, but the Word of God will not make any mistakes. The Word of God has been tried seven times in the furnace of God's holiness and God said it works. So you can trust and depend upon it.

I, or any man of God, could lay hands on you and release a prophetic word, but that prophecy will not come to pass until you do something about it. Prophecy in my experience is like a car without a driver. That car is not going anywhere. God wants you to put actions to the things He has spoken to your heart, or nothing further will happen. In this chapter, I will share with you what actions will do for you. Did you know actions can save your life? They can determine your promotions, and set things in motion in the realm of the spirit. So today, I will share with you what is available to you, and what sets things in motion in the realm of the spirit, when we act upon God's Word.

Doing the Word

"But be ye doers of the word, and not hearers only, deceiving your own selves." James 1:22

The person who hears the Word of God and just says, "Wow, that is good stuff; that is exciting!" but does nothing with it, is like a man who looks into the mirror and later forgets what he looks like. God is saying we have to be a people of action. We have to be people who not only hear the Word of God, but do something about it.

I love my wife, and I always want to find ways to bring joy to her heart. God is like that, too. There are certain things that bring joy to His heart. One of those things is when we hear His Word, and act like He has spoken the truth and is not a liar. When we hear the Word of God and do nothing about it, we are actually telling Him that we don't trust Him. Some folks have more faith in what the devil is saying than what God is saying. They act and talk that way. They will say, "Oh, my back is killing me again!" which demonstrates faith in what the devil is saying rather than believing what God said about healing. Others might say, "The gas prices are so high and the economy is getting worse!" My friend, we don't live by how well the economy is doing. We live by heavenly resources. Did the Bible say that my God shall supply all our needs according to our pay cheques? No! My God shall supply all our needs according to His riches in glory, not according to Wall Street! God has more than enough to take care of all of us.

As I mentioned earlier, there are more than enough resources here on this planet. Furthermore, God can step beyond the earth, and meet your needs from the realm of the spirit. Like I said before, there are trillions of US dollars that will be extracted from Papa God's earth over the next twenty years. However, these things will not happen until we step into action.

Say to yourself now, "I am a person of action!"

A People of Action

"Therefore whosoever heareth these sayings of mine, and doeth them, I will liken him unto a wise man, which built his house upon a rock: And the rain descended, and the floods came, and the winds blew, and beat upon that house; and it fell not: for it was founded upon a rock." Matthew 7:24-25

God wants us to be people of actions. When you act on a *Now Word* from God knowing you cannot fail, that Word will set your miracle into motion. You have prayed and fasted, now move and do something. Your miracle is in your movement.

Sometimes God does not show us the big picture. I am thankful He didn't show it to me! We grow line upon line and precept upon precept, a little here and a little there. As we keep growing, we may have to make some decisions that will shock every fiber of our beings. We sometimes have to do things so radical that our brains wonder what we are doing. To be like Jesus, we will have to make some decisions, step out, and do things we've never done before. If we desire to be a disciple of Jesus, we have to do things that will shock the environment we find ourselves in. And in doing so, we bring Him the greatest joy.

Many people desire to do the work of Jesus, but only a few dare to step into that realm. For example, we see in the Bible how all the disciples had the same opportunity to walk on the water. However, Peter was the only one who acted on the words of Jesus. We must do the same. Those who step out on the Word launch themselves into a realm in God that only a few enter. You can only do this by stepping out of yourself and entering into Him.

You will never know the full extent of the favor of God that is on your life until you do something you've never done before. Years ago, I remember watching Apostle Charles perform many miracles. I wondered if God would use any believer for that, or just some special people. I had heard other ministers say that miracles will happen through you when you're with a man of God, because something rubs off. I discovered there is some truth to that statement, but it is not the whole truth.

When the day came that I held my own miracle service, satan began lying to me. I fought a mental battle with him. The devil kept telling me that God would only use me if I was with my man of God–not by myself. My internal struggle continued as satan said, "Don't do it! Everybody is watching! You cannot have a healing ministry. You are going to make a fool of yourself." There were Christians and non-Christians at the meeting. And that night, I really wanted to find out for myself–would the same God who is working through Apostle Charles also work through me? There comes a point in everyone's life where they need to know for themselves that the Word of God works for them. Not because of what they have heard or learned, but because of what they have experienced. For it is only then that they will become a threat to the powers of darkness.

I called all the deaf and blind people to come to the front for healing. You have to have this boldness of faith! You won't shock God, He already knows what you need. He will just give you a warm welcome into your destiny!

I put my fingers in the ears of a deaf lady and said, "Come out!" Then I said to the lady, "Can you hear me?"

She said, "Can you hear me?" She could hear and was completely healed! That night was a pivotal moment in my life. Since that day, my life and ministry have never been the same. I stepped out of myself and into the fullness of Christ. You may not act exactly like I did, but whatever God has given you to do, just do it. Your resulting testimony will be the springboard to launch you into a new season.

In the Old and New Testaments we see God's people putting their faith into action and accomplishing mighty deeds. In the Old Testament we see Moses, who had a simple rod that caused the Red Sea to be opened. The rod was backed by God. In the same way, when I lay my hands on someone, I know that my hand is backed by Jehovah because in Him I live and move. When I speak, I'm not speaking alone. You may hear my voice, but in the realm of the spirit they hear the voice of God.

I remember reading how one day, Pastor John Osteen's sister lay sick in a coma. John walked into the hospital and said, "You spirit of cancer, loose my sister!" She was healed, and later she told John that she heard the voice of Jesus. John said, "I was the one who spoke."

She said, "No, I heard the voice of Jesus."

Then John had the revelation that when we speak on Earth, God speaks in the spirit realm.

When we speak on Earth, God speaks on our behalf in the spirit realm.

We also see an example of this with the children of Israel. They were trapped against the Red Sea, but they didn't see God, they saw Moses. When Moses stretched out his hand, God blew and opened the Red Sea. Here we see God working with man to produce the supernatural. As I often say, the physical things, or actions, are the children of spiritual things. The physical realm is under the influence of the spiritual realm. The spirit realm is closer than you think, and not far from us. Wherever there is air, the spirit is there. However, you cannot see it until God opens your eyes. You may not see anything happening, but our actions give God access to do certain things. You may not see changes in the natural, but in the spirit, God is still moving.

When God is moving, whatever blockage is in the natural must leave. For those who are sick, the spirit of infirmity must go. Many times, while I am ministering to people, I can see the affecting spirit right beside them. Then, when I rebuke the spirit, the body recovers. So what happened? When the spirit realm is healed, the physical realm will recover. Remember this, the spirit realm is the parent of the physical realm. This is a principal we must understand if we desire to walk with God and rule over satan's kingdom.

An example of this is when I was in the jungles of Uganda. There was a man who was totally paralyzed because of polio. His legs were like sticks. This man would drag himself to the well to get water. I prayed and rebuked the spirit of infirmity, but there was no change. A few weeks after we left town, the man stood up and went for a run. He was able to walk to the well and get his own water! He shocked the entire village. Everyone was talking about the man born paralyzed, who was now walking. A year later, the man came to my crusade and testified. My friend, these are things you need to understand. If you can win in the spirit, you can win in the natural. If you lose in the spirit, no man can help you. Not even God.

Something similar happened in Prince George, a city in Canada. One lady's grandson was totally paralyzed. She came to the crusade, but was disappointed to discover the service was over. However, she saw us later on at a local grocery store and asked us to pray for her grandson. We did, but there was no immediate change. She took him home and set him on the couch. A few minutes later, he got up and started walking. The whole community was shockedThe newspaper headline said, "Prince George Miracle Boy!" Two years later, I saw his grandma again. She said her grandson is still walking. Oh, what a joy it is to serve Jesus!

The Four Lepers

An amazing example of how God and the angels use our actions is found in *2 Kings chapter 7:1-20*.

Benhadad, the king of Syria had besieged the city of Samaria. As a result, the inhabitants were starving and began eating people. Outside the city gate were four lepers who were starving as well. They reasoned their chances of survival might be greater if they took the risk of going to the Syrian war camp and asking for food, rather than languishing outside the gate of Samaria. At dusk, they followed through with their unusual idea and began walking straight toward the enemy. As these four sickly and emaciated men walked, God caused their footsteps to sound to their enemies like a great army with chariots and horses. The terrified Syrians thought the king of Samaria had hired the Egyptians and Hittites to come and destroy them, and they fled with only the clothes on their backs! To the astonishment and delight of the lepers, they found the camp deserted, with all the food and precious riches remaining! You see my friend, God uses our actions of faith because they release something in the spirit realm that brings solutions in the earth.

I'm trying to show you what happens behind the scenes in the realm of the spirit, so you can be confident that your God is for you. Thank God that four seemingly insignificant lepers decided to do something! Overnight, the desperate famine in Samaria was changed into abundance of food, as well as tents, horses, donkeys, silver, gold, and clothing. What we may think is unimportant often proves to be the hinge of destiny, and the instrument of promotion.

You may think your small actions are not important, but God sees them as mighty. He requires your action and movement in order for you to experience His miraculous hand in your life. Your actions may seem insignificant, but they cause big things happen in the spirit realm, and bring solutions in the earth. For example, God used Joseph's gift of dreams and interpretations, and David's five small stones to solve problems for them. Similarly, beloved, God will not over-ride every challenge you face simply because He is God. He needs your actions in order to move on your behalf. Think about how big, powerful and intelligent God is, and yet He did not get you in a choke-hold and force you to accept Jesus, nor did He manipulate you. You accepted Jesus of your own free will. When you said a simple prayer to ask Jesus, the Son of God, into your life, God moved on your behalf in the spirit realm.

I wish that I had been exposed to this teaching when I was first saved! I would have been much further along in the spirit. The secret is that God moves based on our actions, and we are never facing a situation alone. God and His angels are with us.

Jehoshaphat got the Victory

In *2 Chronicles chapter 20*, we are told of how three great nations declared war against Jehoshaphat, king of Judah. King Jehoshaphat was overwhelmed by this and earnestly prayed and sought the Lord, along with all the people of Judah. God then moved on one of the prophets to bring a Word of deliverance to the king. The Word of the Lord spoken through the prophet was that Jehoshaphat and the people should not fear, because God was going to fight this battle for them. Through this story, we can see how important prophetic ministry is! God will not do anything unless He first reveals His intention to His prophets. You may not be called to function in the office of a prophet, but you have a prophetic voice over your own destiny.

"And they rose early in the morning, and went forth into the wilderness of Tekoa: and as they went forth, Jehoshaphat stood and said, Hear me, O Judah, and ye inhabitants of Jerusalem; Believe in the LORD your God, so shall ye be established; believe his prophets, so shall ye prosper." 2 Chronicles 20:20

The prophetic *Now Word* from God was to appoint singers. There are inherent laws in an acted upon *Now Word* which supersede all earthly laws. Think about Jesus! He came from Heaven and nothing on Earth could stop Him. He functioned based on a set of laws that were superior to the earth realm laws, and He could not be stopped. Your ideas are just the same! They come from Heaven, where there are a different set of rules and laws, and they cannot be stopped.

Jehoshaphat consulted with the people and appointed singers, *"... to sing to the Lord and praise Him in their holy (priestly) garments as they went out before the army saying, Give thanks to the Lord, for His mercy and loving-kindness endure forever!" (vs 21, AMP).* As they were singing praises to the Lord in the spirit, God ambushed the enemy's armies with angels. I don't know if those invisible angels smacked the warring armies upside the head, or what happened. What I do know is, they became so confused they all ended up killing each other. While the children of God were singing His praises, their enemies were busy fighting and killing each other! This happened because they acted on the Word of God.

"For the children of Ammon and Moab stood up against the inhabitants of mount Seir, utterly to slay and destroy [them]: and when they had made an end of the inhabitants of Seir, every one helped to destroy another. And when Judah came toward the watch tower in the wilderness, they looked unto the multitude, and, behold, they [were] dead bodies fallen to the earth, and none escaped." 2 Chronicles 20:23-24

There were so many riches among the dead bodies, the people of Judah took three days to carry them all home. This, dramatic change of circumstances happened when God's people followed His instructions.

I have practiced this principle of acting on the *Now Word* of God many times. During the early years of our church ministry, the Lord spoke these words to me, "I would like you to have a thirty day miracle crusade where I can bless My people with My Presence." He then gave me the plan and showed me how to execute the vision. First of all, I was to invite five ministers to speak at this life changing miracle conference. I then called my team together, shared the vision, and we set everything in motion. But there was one problem – no money! I went back to God like any responsible person would, and I informed Him that I had no money to do what He asked me to do. His response was shocking.

He said, "Just do what I asked you to do." Well, my team printed the posters, reserved the five hotel rooms, called the travel agent and priced out the airline tickets. Now, watch what God did! We sent out all the Bible School students to spread news about the miracle services we were having. One man picked our flyer off his car and came to the church. As he walked into the service, he was healed by the power of God. I want you to listen carefully now to what happened behind the scenes of faith. This man's miraculous healing filled him with such joy that he wrote us a cheque for $60,000, so others could be blessed like he was. Then he told me one of the craziest stories I ever heard.

He said the Lord told him that if he would move his family from the United States to Vernon, British Columbia, He would heal him. This man did not even know where Vernon was, and when he checked the map he thought it might be foolish to go that far. However, just like Abraham, he went. God honored His faith by healing him. In response, the man blessed us by paying for the crusade. This is a miracle I will always remember. And all this happened because I obeyed the *Now Word* from God.

Let us review some principles regarding our acting upon the *Now Word* of God:

- Actions are the proof of what we believe.
- The Word has to be qualified by actions.
- Actions free us from idleness and laziness.
- Your actions are a demonstration to God that you recognize His great faith in you.

Action Demonstrates God's Faith in You

Once we recognize that God has faith in us, we become unstoppable. This is because our actions are a demonstration to God that we are aware He believes in us. We have faith in God and that is exciting, but to know and function in the revelation and mindset that God has faith in us is even more exciting. Having this mindset eliminates insecurities, knowing that the Omniscient, Omnipotent, Omnipresent God, the Creator of life and all things, has faith in us. He sees our flaws and mistakes, yet He still believes in us.

I have faith that God will do anything because I am His son. What about you? Have you arrived at that place in God where you no longer question, "Is it me or is it God?" Have you come to a place in your life where you know how much God believes in you? Will you stop believing the lies of the devil that you are a nobody? When you are firmly established in your identity in Christ, you don't think that way anymore; you just accept that you are in Him and He is in you.

All God's children need to spiritually grow to a point in God where He responds to our thoughts and words based on our relationship with Him. We see an example of this in the life of Samuel. The Bible tells us that God, "Let none of his words fall to the ground," (I Samuel 3:19). We too, must learn His principles and walk in obedience, knowing that acting on the Word of God causes us to walk in our son-ship. Your actions should be free from idleness and demonstrate to God that you have recognized His faith in you. When you have this revelation you will enter a more exciting place in your Christian walk, knowing that God trusts you.

Together, let us say now,

"Papa God, I thank You, because I know that You have great faith in me; You trust me."

Talk to Him and freeze that frame. Tell God,

"You have faith in me. You have confidence in me. From today on, I am going to trust that You are leading me and You are the One Who puts inspirations in my mind. You are the One Who is moving through me, and I trust You. Even more exciting, I know that You trust me."

Say together with me now,

"I have a breakthrough grace on my life! When I step out on my dreams, breakthroughs will be my testimony! I have a breakthrough anointing on my life! When I step out on my dreams, breakthroughs will happen for my family!"

Action is one of the most important keys to reprogramming your life for success. You may have all the knowledge in the world, but if you do not apply action, that knowledge will do you no good. No matter how blessed and gifted you are, you will need to work out the greatness located within you.

Do Something with what you Have

Many of us have been taught the truth, mixed with some error. We have been taught that everything in life is about fairness, and therefore sharing wealth is more Godly than obtaining wealth. To this day, there are those who think governments and other agencies should evenly distribute the wealth amassed by the diligent few. They have a sense of entitlement, and so they do not work to obtain wealth for themselves. There is a popular saying, "Give a man a fish and he will eat for a day; teach a man to fish and he will eat for a lifetime," Some people do not like this idea because they want things to be handed to them, without having to do much. For example, they prefer money to come to them with the ease of winning the lottery.

Let us examine the parable of the men with the talents (money). Many of us are familiar with this story, however we will benefit by really understanding the lessons it teaches us about money.

"For the kingdom of heaven is like a man traveling to a far country, who called his own servants and delivered his goods to them. And to one he gave five talents, to another two, and to another one, to each according to his own ability; and immediately he went on a journey." Matthew 25:14-15 (NKJV)

Notice that each person received a talent according to his own ability. Immediately, someone might say, "Okay, the man who received five talents should give at least two of them to the guy who only has one. That way, things will be more equal and fair." Yet the Bible tells us that the way money was distributed to the servants accurately portrays what the Kingdom of Heaven is like. Therefore, we know that sharing the talents equally all around is not how the Kingdom of Heaven operates. Each person has received what they need to work with, according to their ability. From this we see that God expects each person to use what they have been physically given (the talents or money) along with what they were previously given (their natural God-given ability).

The key to reprogramming yourself for success is understanding you already have what you need to become successful. What you have been given may not be wrapped up in shiny paper or presented on a silver platter, but please don't make the mistake of thinking that means it is not something you can use! Many times your talent is something inconspicuous, which solves a problem for someone else. Your job is to do something with it.

Without a doubt, the extraordinary power of action brings success. Zig Ziglar, motivational speaker and business consultant, once wrote: "The major difference between the big shot and the little shot is: the big shot is just a little shot who kept on shooting." When we keep active, circumstances shift and events are set in motion, however they grind to a stop when we lapse into inactivity.

Whether the time seems perfect or not, we are better off to try and fail (even if we fail numerous times), than to not even try once! I always say that until you have failed one thousand times, you are not qualified to quit. My point here is that your action provokes things in the spirit. In fact, your action is what enables you to succeed!

What are the results of inaction? You can spend your entire life doing nothing, and guess what you will receive at the end of it? Nothing! Or, you can focus your attention on your dream and begin gathering all the information you can to help make that dream a physical reality. Then, weigh the facts and decide what action you will take to initiate your vision. Many people remain inactive for fear they might fail. So what if you fail?

Trying something and not succeeding the first time does not make you a failure. On the contrary, failing to act can make you a failure. Please do not allow the fear of failure to influence your actions. If you choose to do nothing, you will fail anyway! There is nothing wrong with taking action! One of the powerful results of action is that it delivers to you a sense of winning. You are partnering with God in doing something to obtain your dreams, rather than just waiting to see what happens.

If you ever feel unsure whether you should take action or not, just consider the consequences. What would happen if you tried and failed? Would that be worse than not trying and having nothing happen? Never leave yourself in a situation where you could say, *I wish I had*, or, *What if?"* Saying, *I wish*, or *what if* are words of failure and they are not for you!

Tell yourself that you will succeed, and then do something to make your ideas happen!

I strongly urge you, never give up! Take action and keep taking action until you succeed, because one thing is sure: you will never achieve success if you do nothing. The power of inaction is failure. The power of action is success.

Confession of a Winner

I am the Prophet of my Destiny, therefore I DECLARE:
I declare this day that I am breaking forth on the left side and the right side. I decree today that though my beginning may be small, my end shall greatly increase. I decree that I cannot be stopped! There is a grace on my life. I cannot be stopped. I will increase; I will expand; I will give birth, to the dreams that God has given me, because His mighty spirit is working in and through me, in Jesus' mighty Name.

CHAPTER TWENTY

BEING POOR YET RICH

"Because you say, "I am rich, and have become wealthy, and have need of nothing," and you do not know that you are wretched and miserable and poor and blind and naked, I advise you to buy from Me gold refined by fire so that you may become rich, and white garments so that you may clothe yourself, and that the shame of your nakedness will not be revealed; and eye salve to anoint your eyes so that you may see." Revelation 3:17-18 (NASB)

Your wealth is a product of your emotional intelligence, not of how much money you have in your bank account. As a pastor I have counseled many so-called rich people who were on the verge of a nervous breakdown. My friend, money is what you have; wealth is who you are, and what you are becoming.

Being poor, yet rich is a concept that I use to illustrate the atmosphere and conditions that I found myself living in as a child. I grew up in extreme poverty. However, many things have changed in my island village since then. It has become quite modernized.

Nevertheless, as I look back at my life, I realize that the principles I learned from my poor village have made me who

I am today. In hindsight, I am so thankful I was born in a little, poor village because I discovered true riches that I would not trade for a million dollars!

While writing this book, I was debating on whether or not to include this chapter. My hesitation was because saying, "I was poor, yet rich" seems like a contradiction to the principles of faith and success. But the more I think about it, the more I realize it is not a contradiction. It is possible to live in poverty, yet be as wealthy as kings. And I want to share my insight with you, to help you reprogram yourself for success.

What success means to me may differ from how you define success. Because of the blood of Jesus, I can be bold and state emphatically that I am a success. I say this, not because of what I have, but because of who I am, and Whose I am. My heart's desire is to motivate and encourage you to become all you were meant to be.

I want to share with you the same three principles I learned from my poor village. As this book comes to a close, I want to leave you with the inspiring thought that certain values and virtues bring true riches. Money will not make you rich, but being wealthy in thoughts, consciousness, attitude, vision, and purpose will bring you into material substance. Here are the lessons I learned that have made me so rich.

Lesson One: Thankfulness Is a Force

Thankfulness is a force that brings many blessings. Really, thankfulness is a Kingdom virtue that will empower you to become rich in God. Many people are rich in stuff, but poor in God. Every time you see a thankful person, you see someone who is very rich.

Thankfulness seems to be a rare virtue in many circles I have been around. I am not intending to judge or criticize anyone here. I am just trying to highlight a great flaw that I have seen in many dear people. My first encounter with this great virtue was in the life of my mom. My mom would sing and dance while she cooked and cleaned. She would sing songs like:

"Count your blessings, name them one by one,
Count your blessings, see what God hath done!
Count your blessings, name them one by one,
And it will surprise you what the Lord hath done."
Johnson Oatman, Jr.

I loved hearing her sing this song. My mama was so thankful because of what the Lord had done. She never complained about the difficulties of life. She was so consumed with her conviction of thankfulness. Looking back at my childhood, I am still baffled at her conviction. How could she say, "Count your blessings?" What blessings? When our monthly income was less than fifty dollars a month, she still found blessings to thank God for! I wondered how she could sing, "Count your blessings, name them one by one," when our bathroom was an outhouse. Our first-class kitchen was made from a stone on the ground, with just a stick to make the fire. There was no electricity, and we did not even have a refrigerator. What do you do in a situation like this? You get very creative. I can remember how we would tie our meat to our roof, just to keep it fresh.

Still, my mama sang. She would have to wash clothes for ten kids with her hands and a washboard. And in the midst of it, I never heard her make one sound of complaint. In the natural, it does not make sense. However, my mama was very rich in thanksgiving and her heart was full of gratitude. She was confident in the Lord's provision. Living in that environment of thankfulness caused something to enter into my spirit. Today, I can see the blessing of Christ all over me. It is so easy for me to be thankful and to see the blessings. I don't need an angel, or even a preacher, to show me the blessings. I can see it, feel it and taste it! When I see my wife and children, I see the blessings. When I see my church and leaders, I see the blessings. Everywhere I look, all I can see are the blessings. This was a gift that was imparted to me by my mother.

Lesson Two: Hard Work Is a Blessing

"Employment is enjoyment." This is something my Dad used to always tell me.

"There will be no laziness in this family," were the words I would hear almost every morning from my Dad. At the tender age of ten, I would wake up at five in the morning just to take care of twelve cattle. I would feed them, and give them water to drink. There were times I would cry because I was so tired. But my Dad would have no mercy on me.

He would simply say, "If you want to be a man, start working. If you want to be a boy, do nothing. If you don't work, you don't eat. Employment is enjoyment." As a result, I would quickly get over myself. As I look back today, I realize how much this amazing quality has helped shape my life. I am so thankful that my dad was a strong man and not a wimp. These qualities that were modeled and taught to me have helped me so much as an adult to deal with life's difficulties and challenges. I remind my children of these lessons whenever they start whining and want to get out of what they were told to do. We are living in a society where people want something for nothing. They want things to be handed to them without a cost. People want resurrection without the crucifixion. No one wants to burn the midnight oil to get something done.

My friend, there are blessings that come from hard work. It is still a virtue that Heaven is attracted to.

Lesson Three: The Virtue of a Strong Family

In the village, your family goes beyond your blood. We had a strong sense of community in the village. My community was not rich in substance, but when one person in the village was hurting, we were all hurting. We shared in everything, sometimes too much. Today, you can live in an apartment for years without even knowing your neighbor's name. I remember how shocking it was for me during my first few weeks in Canada. I would smile and say, "Good morning," a lot. No one would respond. And as a result, people often misunderstood me. For example, in my village, we told everybody we loved them. But when I said that to people in Canada, they got crazy ideas. They saw wedding bells, when I was just trying to greet them. In my village, whether the problem was mine or yours, and regardless of who was at fault, we would do things as a family. There were no spirits of individualism. Stinginess, greed, and self-absorption were seldom in my village.

These are just a few of the virtues I have learned from my poor village. They have taken me places and opened doors for me that would have remained closed, had I not learned them. They have made me who I am today.

As this book comes to a close, I would like to share some testimonies from other people in our ministry whose lives have been transformed by the power of God.

My Breaking Heart Was Healed.

"I could write a book myself about every single thing my husband and I have received as a result of sitting under the ministry of Apostle Everton and Pastor Tracy! I spent the last 20 years and over $250,000 on all manner of new age teaching, looking for more of God everywhere else except in church. Surely the God Who Apostle taught about could not be the God I thought He was when I was a child?

Through the School Of Ministry, Apostle Everton has made the Bible a personal book, written for me. It is alive to me now. I am beginning to live in the fullness of the life God created for me! When I arrived at Living Faith, I still felt like I was on the outside looking in. I felt like I should just be grateful God would even let me back anywhere near Him. So, I accepted whatever bare minimum I believed I deserved. My father passed away when I was two years old, and my mother, just eight years ago. Their deaths succeeded in finally sucking all the joy out of my life. I had given up hope to ever be fully joyful again – I just let it die with them. However, my joy is being restored. I no longer wish for what other people have. The Holy Spirit is also breaking lifelong strongholds in my life. I wake up every day talking to my Father, and declaring my gratitude for all of His promises and blessings on my life! All these things would never have happened without Apostle Everton and his teaching. Our blessing back to him, will be to become as powerful in the Kingdom as he has shown us God wants us to be!"
J.L.

I Am Now Renewed by God.

"I decided to take the first year of the School of Ministry and was very impressed with everything I learned. Yes, I was reborn and saved from the bondage of the enemy, but that didn't stop the enemy from attacking me. That is where the knowledge that I have learned has come in to protect me. Being raised Catholic, I didn't have much of an understanding about what it meant for Jesus Christ to save us and what His sacrifice for us really meant.

But it goes much deeper than this. I have learned how to renew my mind to understand that life is not about accepting and believing what the world has to offer, because we are here to reign, and not suffer. I have learned that through our redemptive rights, we have dominion over this world. Through our actions and faith, the Lord can heal the sick, and protect us in any situation, especially because the enemy has been defeated. Because of the School of Ministry, my life will never be the same, as I'm not just reborn, I'm renewed!"
A.L.

My Insecurity Has Turned into Courage. I am healed.

"I was born and raised in Jamaica. In 2009, I moved to Canada and was alone, I lost sight of who Jesus was, and I no longer had any hope. The first night I came to Living Faith, Prophet Everton spoke life into my dead and hopeless mind, soul and spirit. He prophesied that the curse was broken off my family, and that I am like Queen Esther. These thoughts helped change me. When I first started attended Living Faith, I was a hurt, insecure, girl. However, today I am a beautiful lady who takes pride in herself and wants to become all that God wants for me. I am now empowered to start living out my dreams.

This ministry has impacted me in a powerful way. Apostle Everton has become my spiritual father. He showed me healthy love, which I had never received from a man in my life. That love supernaturally wiped away the hatred I had for men, and removed the negative image I had of my father and step-dad. As

a result, I was able to forgive them. We were able to move on, and now we know each other in such a special way. My spiritual father and mother have aided me to become this person I am today. I have become a daughter of Zion. My heart is committed to growing and establishing the vision for this ministry because of the many testimonies I have, and the new life I now live."
S.W.

My Family Life Has Changed.

"While attending my first meeting at Living Faith, I was touched by the Holy Spirit in my body. I had been diagnosed with arthritis, and that night, the suffering stopped. I also attended the School of Ministry, and my life has never been the same. I discovered the TRUTH about who I am, what I have, and what I can do, because of my personal relationship with God through Jesus Christ.

I have witnessed many people freed from pain, sickness, loneliness, lack and brokenness. For example, my grand-daughter no longer uses a leg brace, my husband was healed from chronic kidney stones and a ten year infection, and our child's life has been released from criminal charges. We have also had so many financial miracles and favour from others.

Christ has done great things in my life through Apostle Everton's ministry."
E.G.

Healed from Fourteen Years of Milk Allergies

"Our son was diagnosed with allergies at six months of age. We were told that his allergies were very rare, and only two per-cent of all children ever outgrow them. One Sunday morning, Apostle spoke a word of prophesy that someone had received healing from their dairy allergies. I remember asking our son in our vehicle as we drove home, "What do you think about what Apostle said in the service?"

His response somewhat took me by surprise as he said, "I receive that!"

On Saturday morning, our son wanted to have our usual pancake breakfast with cow's milk, instead of our usual soy or almond milk substitution. He felt an urge to take a step of faith! That night we celebrated his healing by ordering in pizza for the first time as a whole family! When our daughter, who was not present for the pancake breakfast, saw her brother eating the pizza, she exclaimed, "Are you trying to kill yourself?!" She was amazed to witness him polish off a few pieces of pizza for the first time in fourteen years!

The next day, the enemy tried to steal away the healing. Our son decided he would drink a glass of cow's milk for the first time, to see what it tasted like. He looked at me and said, "Mom, what would have happened right now if I wasn't healed from my allergies?" I proceeded to tell him, and with my nursing history, I was very detailed. He took a few sips of the milk and proceeded to get ready for church. Moments later, he came into our room, quite upset and crying. He felt he was having a reaction. We immediately prayed with him and gave him some anti histamine medication.

Later on, we told Apostle what had happened throughout the week. Apostle said a simple prayer, and said our son would be fine. Since then, our son's allergies have never returned. Praise God! He has indulged in perogies with sour cream, pizza days at school, ice-cream ... and anything else he chooses to eat, with absolutely no bondage to allergies! God is good!"
D. & P. E.

Healed from High Blood Pressure

"Living Faith School of the Supernatural is like no other. With much education already 'under my belt' I wondered, "What more can I learn?" I soon discovered that I can learn quite a lot! I discovered the truth that we are joint-heirs with Christ, and all that He is and has is ours, including authority. As I studied and learned, my faith catapulted to new levels! Meditating on these revelations, I used them as weapons to function in my newly found authority. As a result, a long awaited document was approved and arrived in the mail. I was also healed of high blood pressure. I had been taking medication for ten years. However, during prayer, I heard the words, "Jesus can't have high blood pressure, so neither can you." I am now walking in divine health. Since receiving this teaching, my life has never been the same!"
A.S.

Healed from Migraine Headaches

"Beginning in my early years, I suffered from severe migraine headaches. They began to happen almost daily. The migraines affected my body so that I experienced visual distortions, numbness of my face and hands, and vomiting and dry-heaving, eventually leading to blackouts. I would have excruciating pain in my head that would last up to twelve hours at a time. During these attacks, I could not eat or sleep, leaving me physically weak. Due to the intense pressure and pain in my head, I began to entertain discouraging thoughts which suggested that brain damage might be occurring.

I enrolled in the School of the Supernatural. One day, Apostle Everton was speaking on how, "God is light, and in Him is no darkness at all." (1 John 1:5). Verse seven of that same chapter says, "If we walk in the light as He is in the light, we have fellowship one with another and the blood of Jesus Christ His

Son cleanseth us from all sin." I took that Word with me, and I searched for all the Scriptures I could find on the light and the blood of Jesus. By exposure to the preached Word of God, I gained revelation knowledge, and through meditation on the written Scriptures, the virtue of God healed me. I saw myself as one with God, and every form of darkness left. I have not had another migraine since. Today, I am happily married and serve as one of the worship leaders at Living Faith."
C.W.

My Miracle Baby Boy

"At seventeen weeks pregnant, an ultrasound revealed that I was carrying twins, but that I had lost one. The surviving fetus had omphalocele, (a condition where the abdominal wall was not closed). I was advised by doctors to abort this fetus because the many ultrasounds did not give a positive outlook for this child. We prayed to God, and turned to Apostle Everton and Pastor Tracy, to pray and stand in faith with us for this miracle child. God gave us the faith to hold on, and to trust Him to deliver, despite all the negative ultrasound reports. When our baby was born, he had to have coverings over every orifice of his body to prevent infection, and he had surgery to close his tummy. However, our son pulled through strong; our miracle child was named Edem, meaning Delivered by God. He is now free of the many tubes. Edem is indeed a miracle child and it is all God's doing!"
D. & R. A.

Breakthrough in Employment

"When we came to Vernon, we did not have much money, and were on welfare. Unfortunately, these funds were not enough to physically get by on and feed the both of us. So, we prayed. We had heard somewhere that you did not have to pay tithes on welfare cheques, so we didn't because we were afraid that we wouldn't have enough money to live on.

Then one service, the message came forth from Apostle on tithing; that if we would put the Lord first by paying our tithes to Him, He would open up the windows of Heaven and keep the devourer from us. The Lord said, "Try Me and see what I will do."

So, we tried the Lord and started to pay tithes. True to His word, He opened up the windows of Heaven and He poured out more than a blessing. He poured out abundance, more blessings than our little apartment could hold, and more food than we could eat. Favor was surrounding us everywhere. I found a job, and I was faithful in that job. Even when other employee's hours got cut back, I was increased to full-time work. Then my wife got a job too, not just one offer but two. We held God to His word in time of need and our needs were always met. I believe we are under an umbrella of covenant blessings and protection, because we are connected to this body of believers and to Apostle Everton and Pastor Tracy. I am thrilled to say that God is changing lives! There is a domino effect where, if one member of the body rejoices, the rest of us rejoice!"
D. & J. E.

My Miracle Baby

"In November 2012, Apostle Everton was at our church in Switzerland and had a word about, "Something spectacular out of the womb in the month of February; something divine for you two," and to, "Go into prayer; go into fasting." The prophecy was actually directed at someone else, but my husband and I both felt strongly that this was the answer we were praying for about our next child. On our way back home that night, we talked about it. We felt it would be a boy, and decided to call him Everton. In the next two months I spent twenty days

fasting, and many hours with God daily. To make a long story short, we conceived in February! Because God spoke a lot about giving us a double blessing, we thought they were twins. But in the end, God explained to us that it is one child: one double blessing! As we know about the covenant friendship of Apostle Everton and Apostle Charles, we named him Everton Charles. He is our spectacular double blessing from God!"
J.H.S.

I Found my Divine Purpose.

"Through this ministry, I found something that my soul longed for; divine purpose. I never knew that I could speak in front of crowds, especially since the majority of people are scared stiff of public speaking, myself included. I never thought I would one day stand up in a prison in Nigeria and give a speech to prisoners, or speak to a group of men in India (where they separate the men from the women), and then have the men applaud. I found my insides were stretched to my very core, demanding the very best to come out of me, and it did. I recognized I have much to give the world in whatever profession or mission I am working on, or even whatever hobby or past-time I am doing.

Because of this ministry I have been equipped with spiritual and practical tools in order to succeed in whatever I set my hands to do. Today, I find myself in a job that I never would have entertained before. I love it. I would have never have considered myself qualified, but I know the One who qualifies me. I am right where I am supposed to be."
M.A.

I Have my Fight Back.

"After connecting with Apostle Everton and Pastor Tracy's ministry I have seen an immense shift in my life personally, spiritually and in the realm of business. The anointing upon their ministry is unmatched, and they have imparted wisdom and anointing to me through their incredible teaching.

I have had incredible breakthrough in personal finances and divine connections to business people. As well, I have experienced personal healing and growth in the last two years, where for many years, I could not seem to get breakthrough.

When I first connected to the Weekes' ministry, I was discouraged, wounded, and had no passion for Jesus anymore. I was a wounded soldier. Now my thinking has changed, not only about myself personally, but also about my spiritual calling and my divine potential in business. I am now walking in divine confidence, which is opening new doors for relationships, as well as business opportunities.

I have personally come to know Jesus and the price that He paid for me through His redemptive work on the cross. I am learning to walk in the dominion that I was created to walk in.

These incredible teachings through the School of the Supernatural, Apostle Weekes' book, *The Cleansing Blood*, his teachings on success, and the personal mentorship of Apostle Everton and Pastor Tracy have given me deeper passion and new fire for Jesus.

I am forever grateful to them both for the love they share with me, their wisdom, anointing, and their faith in my family and I and our future."
D.P.

PRAYER FOR SALVATION
AND
BAPTISM IN THE HOLY SPIRIT

Heavenly Father, I come to You in the Name of Jesus. Your Word says, "Whosoever shall call on the name of the Lord shall be saved" (Acts 2:21). I am calling on You. I pray and ask Jesus to come into my heart and be Lord over my life according to Romans 10:9-10. "If thou shalt confess with thy mouth the Lord Jesus, and shalt believe in thine heart that God raised him from the dead, thou shalt be saved." I do that now. I confess that Jesus is Lord, and I believe in my heart that God raised Him from the dead.

I declare that I am now reborn! I am a Christian - a child of Almighty God! I am saved! Jesus, you also said in Your Word, "If ye then, being evil, know how to give good gifts unto your children: How much more shall your heavenly Father give the Holy Spirit to them that ask him?" (Luke 11:13). I'm also asking You to fill me with the Holy Spirit. Holy Spirit, rise up within me as I praise God. I fully expect to speak with other tongues as You give me the utterance (Acts 2:4).

Begin to praise and thank God for filling you with the Holy Spirit. Speak those words and sounds you receive—not in your own language, but the heavenly language given to you by the Holy Spirit. You will have to use your own voice, because God will not force you to speak.

Now you are a Spirit-filled believer. Continue with the blessing God has given you and pray in tongues each day. You'll never be the same!

If you have prayed this prayer, please let us know. We would like to send you soem literature that will help to strengthen you in your new walk with Jesus!

Worship

with us at

Living Faith Miracle Center

Living Faith Miracle Center is a charismatic church in Kelowna and Vernon. The services at Living Faith have been designed with you in mind. Our meetings are family orientated and full of the life, love and power of God.

We offer uplifting music; powerful teaching that is relevant to the issues you face in life and dynamic programs for children of all ages. If you need prayer or someone to talk to, our leadership team is available to minister to you after each service.

Come and worship with us as we experience the presence of God in a friendly and safe atmosphere.

Living Faith

Mending Lives Giving Purpose

Living Faith Miracle Center
One Church - Multiple Locations
1551 Water St., Kelowna, BC Canada
250-763-2993   www.mlmi.org

have helped thousands of people come into victory and purpose in Christ. As they hold cutting-edge Teaching Seminars and Miracle Crusades all over the world, the Gospel is demonstrated with undeniable proofs.

The call of God and the mandate on their lives has provoked them to travel to many nations as Pastors, Evangelists, Teachers, Ministers of Healing, and Church Planters. Apostle Everton and his teams travel the nations of the world bringing refreshing and healing to God's precious people.

Their ministry is characterized by a powerful manifestation of the gifts of the Spirit, and through these gifts the principles of faith, victory and apostolic revelation are conveyed to the Body of Christ. God has commissioned them to heal the sick, win the lost, plant churches, establish training centers, and to raise up a new generation of world-changers that walk daily in the power of God.

As they pursue in Ministry with excellence and passion, lives are being transformed by the glorious Gospel.

At present, Apostle Everton and Tracy Weekes are the Founders and Senior Pastors of the Living Faith Miracle Centers, both in Kelowna and Vernon, B.C. They are also the Presidents of Miracle Life Ministries International and currently preside over the School of the Supernatural, which is growing exponentially every year.

Apostle Everton and Pastor Tracy Weekes are a couple after God's own heart who dare to believe God's Word! They are a powerful husband and wife team and the proud parents of four beautiful children, all of whom are their great delight.

OUR MISSION...

To train up a generation of believers
who walk daily in the power of God

Do you desire to be
used of God to bring healing
and deliverance to your world?

Enroll today in the School of the Supernatural
Where normal believers are transformed into world changers!
www.sosn.org   Email: apostle@lfmc.tv
Call for more info: 1-250-763-2993

The Program of Study

Our vision is to train up men and women of God who walk daily in the power of God. The curriculum includes courses in four major sections: Bible Knowledge, Charismatic Theology, Kingdom Business, and School of the Apostles and Prophets. Upon completion of the program, you will be equipped with the knowledge and skills necessary to be an effective minister for the Gospel of Jesus Christ.

What you will receive upon completion of the 11 course program:

Certificate in Biblical Studies
Opportunities to travel with, and be mentored by Apostle Weekes
Potential to become a licensed Minister (pending further evaluation)

·Power of Redemption
·Activating Your Redemptive Imagination
·Dominion of the Believer

·Understanding Your Divine Purpose
·The Anointing for Success
·Setting the Captives Free
·The Christ Life
·Kingdom Business 1

Life Changing Teachings by Apostle Everton Weekes

Sale: $20
THE CLEANSING BLOOD OF CHRIST
In this living masterpiece get ready to learn:
·How to use the blood of Jesus against the powers of darkness

·The nine Wonders of the Blood

·Why satan is so afraid of the Blood of Jesus

·Keys on how to take refuge in the blood of Jesus

·Why there is still power in the blood

Sale: $50
HAVE FAITH IN GOD'S GREAT LOVE
Get ready to receive healing and become all that God desires you to become. As you do, you will receive a revelation of God's love for you, that will bring a revolution to your world!

10 Part series available in CD or MP3

Sale: $30
THE GREAT PHYSICIAN

In this life changing teaching, Apostle Everton Weekes will introduce you to the Great Physician. For over 2000 years, Jesus has not lost one case. Get ready to be healed and to be restored.

6 Part series available in CD or Mp3

Sale: $30
POWER OF THE BLESSING
Do you know that there is power available to bring you into true riches? When you made Jesus the Lord over your life, He not only saved you from the power of sin, but brought you into the realm of blessing.